the crossing project

living, dying and transformation in Banaras

SACRED WORLD FOUNDATION

San Francisco

www.sacredworld.com

One of the world's first examples of physical-virtual icons developed at Kondapalli, Andhra Pradesh, India. c. 1998.

Living, Dying & Transformation in Banaras

The Crossing Project

Ranjit Makkuni and Madhu Khanna

SACRED WORLD FOUNDATION

San Francisco

www.sacredworld.com

First published by Sacred World Foundation, 2003
Sacred World Foundation
2130 Fillmore Street, # 110
San Francisco, CA 94115

ISBN : 81-88934-14-3

Printed in India by
M/S Neographics
K-2071 (first floor),
Chittaranjan Park, New Delhi-110019.

Catalogue Design
Tarun Rawat

Distributed in India by:
Sharada Publishing House
40, Anand Nagar, Idrerlok
Delhi - 110035

contents

FOREWORD

When one thinks of a guru, one immediately pictures an image of the Buddha in orange robes sitting under a banyan tree, expounding knowledge. During my tenure at Xerox Palo Alto Research Center (PARC), I encountered many gurus. They were not all dressed in orange robes, but their mentorship was just as intense as the orange-robed gurus under the banyan trees in India.

It is a great honour that the Crossing Project has been nurtured under the umbrella of modern teachers, John Seely Brown and Per-Kristian Halvorsen. John and Per-Kristian were the pioneers who recognized that Silicon Valley may not be the only centre of technological innovation, and pushed us to shift our perspective to the rest of the world. It was their vision that led me back from PARC to India, and discover the great richness of Banaras.

I would like to thank Carlos Pascual for the commitment of Xerox Developing Markets Operations in establishing a world-class research laboratory in India, The Crossing Media Lab. In addition, I value the support provided by Rajiv Batra and Khurshid Bandopadhyaya of Xerox India, for extending their visionary support to the project, especially when the world was englobed in financial recession.

Moving forward simultaneously on the design, technology and content vectors of the Crossing Project's research, in a short span of time, has been an immense challenge. From the early stages, Dr. Madhu Khanna contributed to the research and later joined me as a close collaborator, and provided her library, and the necessary space to manifest our creativity. Within moments after a sizzling discussion on radio-frequency tags with Roy Want and Anuj Gujar at PARC, we found ourselves in an ancient village in Kondapalli, South India, renowned for toys and we were on to building the world's first physical virtual icons and tangible interfaces (see cover flap).

These prototypes formed the basis of our technology and design efforts. Over the two years of The Crossing Media Lab, many artists, designers, craftsmen, multimedia programmers, videographers have passed through its doors, but I would like to highlight the contributions of my close collaborators, Mustafa Siddiqi, Muralidhar Swarangi, Kalpana Subramanian, Tarun Rawat and Pallab Chakraborty. They provided strong pillars of support, which allowed the project to cover immense horizontal ground in the emerging field of interaction design and Banaras content within a short span of two years.

Each object designed in the Crossing Project cut through a rich spectrum of disciplines from "ritual to robotics" covering the fields of technology, art history, visual and performing arts, crafts, embedded systems designs, multimedia programming, and videography.

My access into Banaras was provided by Mapu Singh. In one stroke, Mapu introduced me to the entire gamut of researchers of Banaras and its spiritual practitioners. I am grateful to the Mahantji of the Kashi Vishvanath Temple,

Banaras, for introducing me to the creation myths underlying the eternal city as well as providing me the short cut through the maze of Banaras' streets to see the divine vision of "Shiva" at the Vishvanath Temple on the crowded Shivratri festival.

In 2001 - 02, in India the project was exhibited twice in Delhi, in Mumbai and Bangalore, and with each showing we recognized increasing endorsement by people for the need to have an Indian signature of design, bridging ancient aesthetics and modern computational tools. I thank Khurshid Bandopadhyaya for her encouragement in ensuring that the contributions and value of this project reach all strata of society through the media, especially underprivileged children.

In 2002, the project was transferred from the Xerox PARC to the Sacred World Foundation. I thank Herve Gallaire, Dave Robson and Mark Stefik for ensuring a smooth transition, so that the value of the project travels beyond just the walls of Xerox PARC to the world.

The Crossing Project has been realized in the context when increasing attention is being devoted to the creation of technologies to heal the digital divide. In this sense, the Crossing Project will serve as an important benchmark in design, so that any new products and tools designed for developing societies will have to compete against such a benchmark.

The project is also situated in the context of richer experience with computing in a modern techno-society. Like prayer beads of the traditional society, where through traditional haptic communications the devotee is in touch with higher realms, the mobile devices of the Crossing Project fulfils our need to be engaged with our hands and bodies, and being engaged in tactile computation.

Instead of holding and interacting with rectangular, inorganic objects characteristic of modern work practice, the Crossing Project restores the value of being in "touch" with forms of our cultural idealizations: The Bodhisattva Avalokiteshwara holds the wishfulling jewel, the Goddess Tara holds a lotus flower in her hand, and the Goddess Ganga holds a pot. Many people from India and the US have held the Crossing objects. I thank you all for your support, for by touching the Crossing objects, you touched a vision to restore beauty in our info delivery devices, and for a moment you became divine visionaries like Avalokiteshwara, Tara and the Goddess Ganga.

New Delhi — Ranjit Makkuni

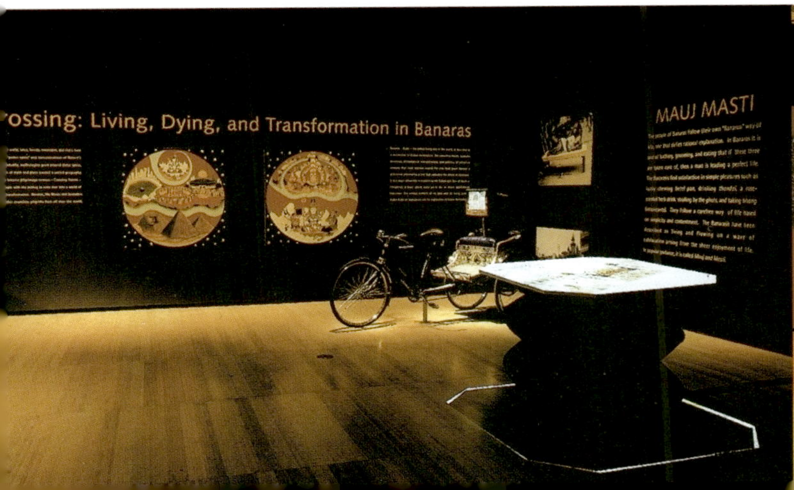

Did the information society do away with the hands?

Against the backdrop of modern, mobile multimedia computing, we present a vision of how the time-tested visions of developing nations and ancient living cultures can shape the form of future information technology. Just as the Internet is a symbol of modern society's notion of connection, in traditional societies, large gatherings around a physical and psychical centre, such as pilgrimages illustrate an alternative, but time-tested notion of interrelationships and connections. Images of a large group of worshippers coming down the Banaras ghats and collectively dissolving in the river Ganga represent a vision of man's relationship with nature at the larger level. In contrast, modern society's mobile computing is yet another notion of distributed connection in a secular environment. The Crossing Project intersects these two to create a new form of art.

The Crossing Project explores alternate paradigms of information access, integrating the hand and the body in the act of computer-based communication and learning. With respect to pilgrimage, the project brings to focus a traditional society's notion of eco-cosmic connection through multimedia technology-based connections. With respect to design, it incorporates the skills of traditional crafts in the design of expressive information devices.

Rich as the images displayed by modern computing are, the act of interacting with the computer has essentially disembodied the user. The Crossing Project, hence, is questioning a 30-year-old assumption: the invention of GUI fundamentally created a separation of the hand and eye. Yet, all the arts teach us that the hand and eye are in an inseparable relationship. The calligrapher's brush, the sitar player's stroke, the dancer's gesture all illustrate the integral hand-eye relationship. If we are to recognize that the artist is that person who displays intelligence in both intellect and the body, and one who is fully expressive with his body, then body is central to the act of communication and interaction. It is precisely this connection modern information technology has lost. Chinese calligraphy shows us how the gesture is visible on the painting, and from the sitar tone we can deduce the plucking gestures of the artist.

Given such a central role for the hands, we ask: Did the information society do away with the hands?

Banaras - Kashi - the oldest living city in the world, is described as a microcosm of Indian civilization. The countless myths, symbolic meanings, philosophical interpretations, and patterns of collective memory that have accrued around the city have given Banaras a distinctive personality, a city which englobes the whole of existence. It is a place where life is relished to the fullest, and fear of death is conquered, and where many choose to die to attain spontaneous liberation. Banaras also represents a meeting of the dimension of intellect and the heart. Spirituality is the great leveler, for in Banaras all are equally naked in the dip in the Ganga. The unique context of Banaras' past and its living present makes Kashi an appropriate domain for the exploration for future technology.

Images of a large group of worshippers coming down the Banaras ghats and collectively dissolving in the Ganga river represent a vision of man's relationship with nature at the larger level. In contrast, modern society's mobile computing is yet another notion of distributed connection in a secular environment. The Crossing Project intersects these two to create a new form of art.

The GUI created the desktop computing paradigm, which, in turn, led to the design of the present form of learning system: the learner interacts with a digital document presented on a workstation using hardware (television monitor, keyboard and mouse), and software (button pushing, windows and point and click).

However impressive the present forms of display technology and speed of information transfer may be, important aspects relating to the physical dimensions of Man have been overlooked by the modern workstation. The workstation disembodies the learner. Presentations become "screen-centric". The workstation becomes the focus of people's offices and homes. While the bits on the computer screen are animated and rich, the learner's body is usually static. Interaction is reduced to button-pushing while the expressive potential of the human hand is completely ignored. The sense of touch is reduced to mere mouse-clicks. Despite the hundreds of hand positions that are possible, interactions with current learning systems are reduced to point and click and button-pushing.

Given that a considerable amount of time of modern man is spent with devices, and that our bodies are continuously engaged with computing, we ask: How do we restore gestures to provide kinaesthetic forms of interaction with digital content? What are the relations between the forms of hand-held interfaces corresponding to the dimensions and spaces created by the hand and body? How can we incorporate the attributes of texture, palpability, tactility in the design of hand-held interfaces? Can the hardware of modern information delivery devices share the burden of communication?

Hence, thirty years after the invention of GUI, we re-question GUI, and reexamine the relationship of the human body to physical interfaces with digital media. We explore new bridges between physical and virtual spaces, new graspable, touchable, adornable interfaces to give users kinaesthetic contact with the learning content.

THE TECHNO-TRADITIONAL MAN DIVIDE: *Towards Cultural Computing*

In our contemporary world, there is a lot of interest in creating new markets in developing nations, and within those nations, bringing computation to new markets in villages. While it will be amazing for a villager to experience the magic of computing, couldn't we ensure that we don't accidentally dump "black and beige" boxes, or dump windows into the developing societies. The products and interfaces developed by the Crossing Project serve as a benchmark for the standards for computing in a traditional society.

Ancient cultures relate to nature differently. Kalidas, the great poet, saw clouds as a love messenger. To 12th century India, the dark clouds were seen as symbols of fertility. Notion of desktop, and "point and click" overlapping windows re-inforce the divide. Building computing tools for developing cultures requires a total re-thinking of the notion of the User Interface.

Does button-pushing apply to nature-based cultures? If we can realize that traditional societies have a well-established, time-tested aesthetic and technical base, can the aesthetics and values of traditional societies and developing nations shape the form of modern computing tools?

In order to create a language of computing appropriate for traditional societies, the Crossing Project deconstructed GUI and evolved a space of interaction exploring gestures, and body-friendly and mythology-friendly forms. Culturally reflective computing may be an important key in making technology accessible across the divide. Designing at the edge of material and mythological dimensions is a way to ensure that technology is accessible to a great majority of people.

The Crossing Project suggests a new generation of cultural computing, but its relevance goes beyond developing nations to include modern techno-society as well. Traditional societies teach us the important perceptions of the body and how postures and gestures, and the practice of art can invoke states of well being and healing.

Building bridges between traditional and technological man

How might traditional craftspersons and artists of traditional societies shape the forms of technology? The Crossing Project aims to illustrate bridges between traditional and techno-man, reconciling orthogonal dimensions. The process of mass-producing information readers and devices itself is at odds with the personalization process of craft creation. For the traditional craftsperson each object has a right to be, and is highly "situated" in contrast to depersonalized "black and biege" boxes characteristic of technological tools.

In a traditional society art making was intimately related to nature. In modern society, technology has become second nature. The world's first display screens were the sky and trees, the human face and hands. Can we learn from the perceptions, skills and talent in traditional society to achieve a synthesis between traditional and modern forms of design?

The world's first user interface designers were craftspeople. Their work carries sophisticated notions of "narrative", notions of time and space, and notions of tactility and touch. Given the high concentration of arts, crafts and "analogue" talent in developing nations, perhaps the next computing innovation may arise from traditional societies. They may provide us that valuable second chance to get "computing right" and achieve a synthesis between modern and traditional cultures.

RANJIT MAKKUNI

Throughout the world, lakes, forests, mountains, and rivers have been seen as "power spots" and concentrations of nature's energies. Gradually, mythologies grew around these spots, and the union of myth and place created a sacred geography. They became pilgrimage centres - *Crossing Points* - providing people with the setting to cross over into a world of healing and transformation. Banaras, like Mecca and Jerusalem, represents a sacred centre pilgrimage power spot.

Banaras - Kashi - the oldest living city in the world, is described as a microcosm of Indian civilization. The countless myths, symbolic meanings, philosophical interpretations, and patterns of collective memory that have accrued around the city have given Banaras a distinctive personality, a city which englobes the whole of existence. It is a place where life is relished to the fullest, and fear of death is conquered, and where many choose to die to attain spontaneous liberation. The unique context of its past and its living present makes Kashi an appropirate choice for the exploration for future technology.

In the course of day-to-day dissolution Hara...lifts up his own city at the tip of his trident and holds it aloft. Hence, Kashi is devoid of the ravages of Time and Death.

Skanda Purana, Part 4 Section 1. Chap.30, Verse110.

KASHI *the city of faith*

The theme of the Crossing Project is Banaras - Kashi - the oldest living city in the world in its multifaceted aspects, described as a microcosm of Indian civilization. When we "read" a culture of a city, whether ancient or modern, we are speaking not only about the physical geoscape of the city but about people and their abstractions with which they define their self-identity and worldview. Banaras, as it stands today, is an urban patchwork of different communities who live in mohallas and narrow lanes or "galis", some too narrow for even a buffalo to cross. Like most ancient cities in India today, Banaras too, is plagued by its share of urban decay. However, this grim outer facade has to be complemented by an understanding of the way in which urban dwellers over there personalize or transgress their immediate environment by perceiving their religious city in ways different from other secular environments.

Ancient historiography reflects that Banaras has several names. The names exemplify multiple dimensions of the city. In primeval times, Banaras was described as an idyllic forest paradise — a Forest of Bliss or "Ananda Vana", with green groves, pools and streams anointed with the droplets of heavenly Ganga, abundant with nectarine water. The name, Kashi, is one of the oldest names of the city. In the *Kashi Khanda (26.67),* it is stated that since light emanating from Lord Shiva shines here, let its other name be Kashi. Thus, Kashi is that city which illumines the path to spiritual liberation. It is, therefore, referred to as the "City of Light." In the *Buddhist Jatakas* and the *Mahabharata,* Banaras is called Varanasi, which derives its name from the two rivers, Varana in the north, and Asi in the south, that embrace the city. The two rivers are the boundaries of the sacred circuit. The crescent-shaped river bank is girded by the two rivers and the tract of land between them is the best place for a pilgrimage. Another significant name is Avimukta, "The Never Forsaken" territory of Lord Shiva, who explains "because I never foresake it, nor do I let it go. This great place is, therefore, known as Avimukta." This emphasizes the fact that Shiva is eternally present here and people should never leave it. The place is permeated with the invisible presence of Shiva. So Kashi has the distinction of transforming all those who are there into the likeness of Shiva. Hence, living in Kashi one becomes *Rudramaya* "identical with the essence of Shiva". On account of this association, Kashi is known as Rudravasa or a place where Rudra lives. In the *Skanda Purana,* Kashi is also referred to as, The Great Cremation Ground or the Mahashmashana because at the end of the cosmic cycle, Kashi is considered to be the spot that absorbs the corpse of the entire universe composed of the five elements within its fold.

Shiva holding the city of Kashi on his trident.
Orissa style centrepiece.

Kashi is not simply civic units but a religious unit. The religious boundaries of the city have changed over a period of time. The *Padma Purana* describes the shape of the city from time to time. In ancient times, Kashi was balanced on Shiva's trident. Thereafter, its boundary was a circle of ten miles radius; later the eastern side of the Ganga was cut down to a chariot shape. Thereupon, the boundary was reduced to the north, and resembled the shape of a conch. It is around this shape that the Panchakrosi circumambulation of the city is performed. According to Kuber Natha Sukul (1974:9), this variation of size and shape has historical roots.

There are two interconnected Kashis. A multi-religious city in time and history - a city observed by non-Hindus where people, like anywhere else, live and earn. Culturally, Kashi is a melting pot of class, race and social communities. It is one of the foremost cultural and spiritual capitals of India generating change, as much as timeless continuity. The other, is the Kashi of the Hindu imagination, a city outside time and

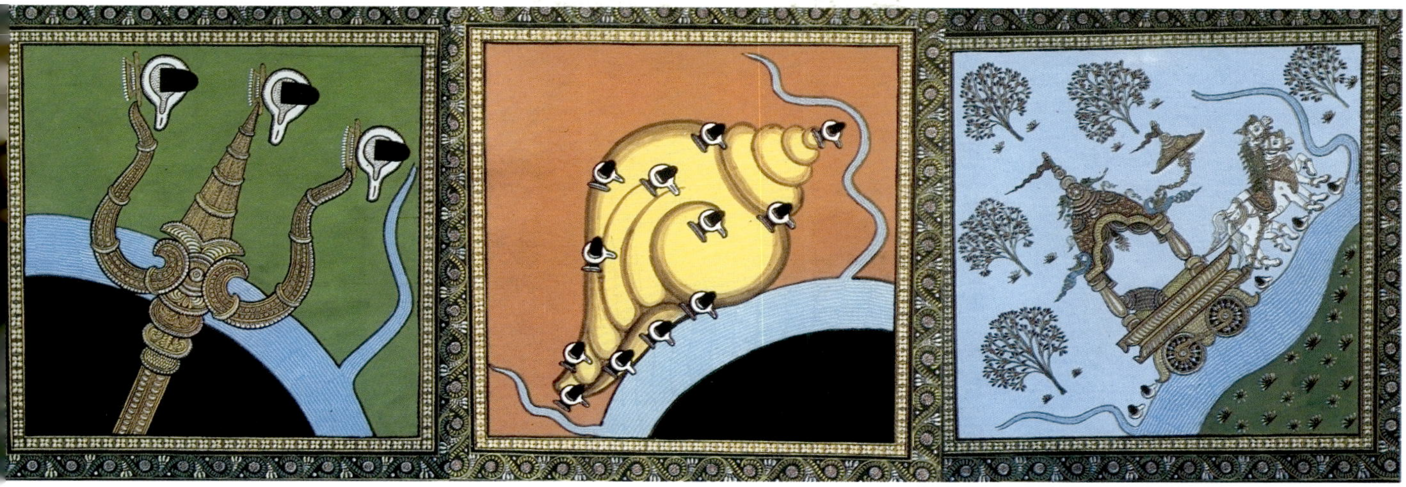

The mythical representations of Kashi through the four *yugas*.

history shaped by multiple layers of mythical history and philosophical symbolism, where people from all over India come for spiritual rewards. The tradition of modern thought is analytical, objective, impersonal, determinate, individualistic; also in large measure, it is inspired by a mechanistic worldview of life. In contrast, the traditional worldview, such as the one represented in Banaras, draws from collective memory of spiritual experiences, derived from direct insight (*darshana*) and value-oriented transcendental truths rooted in man-cosmos unity. Hence, to describe Kashi merely as an ancient city "older than legend and history", as Mark Twain did, is to understate its significance. In Hindu imagination, Kashi is not perceived as a physical landscape. It is, in essence, a faithscape, an amphitheatre of ancient gods and goddesses of the Hindu pantheon, and the subliminal powers of water spirits and elements. This other-worldliness allows for a certain fluidity of perception and of contrasting ethos. In Kashi, life and death go arm in arm. One can never tell where reality ends and illusion begins, where the sacred and the profane meet and part and where life's fleeting joys and sorrows intersect with the idea of joyful death. In this scenario death loses its sting and life flows swiftly changing its colours like the river Ganga through the seasons.

The multiple richness of Banaras invokes many different interpretations. The most significant of them is that Kashi is the greatest of all *tirthas*, or a pilgrimage site described as a "crossing place" from the material realm to the transcendental plane which frees the agent from the repeated round of births and deaths. People from all over India come to Kashi because it is this envisioned "centre" of the cosmos, that acts as a doorway "or a ford" between earth and heaven. Pilgrims go on a sacred journey or a *Kashiyatra* that modifies all acts and impresses them with special signification. The pilgrimage to

Kashi is not an ordinary journey; it involves interaction with sacred sites. At a subtle level, a *tirtha yatra* or a pilgrimage to Kashi involves interaction with specific sites, relics, architecture, holy idols, sacred narration, and symbolic gestures, guided by sacred paths and geographies of the symbolic landscape. The aura of divine presence envelopes Kashi much more than any other place. It is said that when Brahma weighed the sky with its gods against Kashi, Kashi being heavier on account of the merits it bestows to all sank down to earth, and the sky soared above. (*Skanda Purana* 4.1.30.89).

It is believed that Kashi is outside historical-consciousness. Jonathan Parry in his work (1993: 106-7) explains the meta significance of the holy Kashi. Untouched by the shifting pulsations of time or the processes of destruction that takes place on earth, it is conceived to be different from all other cities - a place untouched by the temporal flow of time. Thus, according to traditional perception, Kashi stands apart from all the envisioned spheres of the Hindu cosmos: the three *lokas* (heaven, earth and netherworld), fourteen worlds or the nine regions of the envisioned cosmos. That is to say, it contains within its radius, all the spheres of the cosmos. Since Kashi encompasses all spaces, a circumambulation of the city is equated with the circumambulation of the cosmos. Not only is Kashi the greatest of all *tirthas* or pilgrimage sites, by the same intuitive logic, the ebb and flow of time in Kashi is considered to be eternally auspicious. It is commonly held that: "It is always Satayug, the Golden age in Kashi". The three temporal powers, Yama, the god of death, his emissary and the Kaliyuga, have no jurisdiction there. Even aeonic time cannot reach it; fixed as a pole star, Kashi is raised high above. In the timeless city there is no *karmic* retribution. Therefore, all who live there within its circuit have spontaneous access to spiritual release (*moksha*). A well-known image of the city shows Shiva holding the city on his trident at the time of cosmic dissolution (*pralaya*). Kashi survives the holocaust! The countless myths, symbolic meaning, philosophical interpretation, and patterns of collective memory that have accrued around the city have given Banaras its distinctive identity.

If one were to visualize a map of India's spiritual currents, all the energy lines will converge into Kashi. For, Kashi gathers together in its landscape the whole of the Indian spiritual cosmos. Kashi is called a *mandala* of all the pilgrimages of the cosmos. In a symbolic sense, this *tirtha* contains in a single location all the 33 crore gods of the Hindu pantheon who are enchanted by its brilliance and spiritual potency; all the seven sacred centres of all India (*sapta puris*); and the four famous sacred abodes (*dhams*). In Kashi, the 12 *jyotirlingas* located in different parts of India are all found here. It is this centrifugal nature of the pilgrimage city that makes it a "cosmopolis" and a microcosm of Hindu culture. For these reasons, it is considered to be a place so holy that one does not need to do anything there— "just being there is a yoga".

Whatever touches Kashi, that thing becomes her, just as a stream of wine poured into the river Ganges becomes like the Ganges. Just as iron touching the philosopher's stone becomes gold, so does one obtain the very form of Brahman, which is the form of Shiva, in Kashi. Kashi Rahasya Chap.14, Verses 40-41.

Like a crystal, this luminous city refracts its sparkling rays outside its boundaries. Thus, according to Hindus several sacred cities, such as Uttar Kashi, the Kashi of North India in the northern Himalaya, and Shiva Kashi in South India replicate the archetypal Kashi. It is held that Lord Vishvanath travelled all the way to Puri in Orissa to praise Lord Jagannath and stayed there in a small shrine in the compound of the Jagannath temple complex. Similarly, there are smaller villages like Kashipur in the northeast, which embody the original city. These spots offer the same benefit that one enjoys in Kashi.

As early as the second century B.C., the multiple qualities of the sacred city - its natural beauty, its flora and fauna, its commercial significance and a place that ensured spiritual salvation and knowledge of truth was recognized. The unique context of its past and its living present makes Kashi the most appropriate subject for exploration for future technology. The Crossing Project exhibit consists of a collection of installations and interfaces that allows one to experience and access the multi-layered aspects of Kashi. The multi-media exhibit is divided into six sections: from the streetscape where life is celebrated in typically "Banarasi" ways to the notions of Shiva and Ganga and from the sacred geography of the ghats to the sublime notion of death in Kashi.

MADHU KHANNA

SPOKEN EN
COMPETITIVE EXAMS.

Cycle Jhalla

The cycle jhalla is a lyrical video installation based on the cycle rickshaws of Banaras. The installation looks at the musical, playful, chaotic nature, and visual aesthetic of the rickshaw in the streets of Banaras. It is inspired from the concept of the "jhalla", a term used to describe a kind of intense musical progression in Indian instrumental music forms.

The spokes of the wheel relate to the steel strings of the sitar and this installation establishes a correspondence between the spokes of the wheel and the sitar. Through an aural backdrop of five sitar jhalla compositions, this section intended to capture the movement, rhythm, geometry and colour of the cycle rickshaw which is visualized as a poetic relief on the Banaras cityscape, a musical instrument in itself.

The cycle rickshaw is a popular living symbol of the Banarasi way of life. Rickshaws in Banaras have their own special identity. Vividly decorated, they have peculiar high and sloping seats and special brass bells tied at the back. The shopkeeper at one of the oldest rickshaw shops will tell you that the rickshaw came to Banaras about 1940. Before this, the main mode of transport was the *ikka* or the horse cart. Till this day the cycle rickshaw has continued to be the most popular and eco-friendly means of road transport in Banaras.

The rickshaws, besides being a mode of transport, are a work of art. Their shining steel form is branded with colourful motifs and decorated with tassels and bells. The bell is a special feature. It is made of a brass that produces a clear ringing sound when struck. This is probably one of the few cities in the world where a traffic jam can be pleasant to the ears. The orchestra of ringing bells at Gadaulia Chowk is a regular feature in the evenings.

The cityscape is a patchwork of quaint old temples, crumbling houses and a multitude of small shops tightly sewn together leaving lanes, like narrow seams between them. These lanes allow a traffic of people and cows to squeeze past each other. The rickshaws bounce along these bumpy lanes miraculously avoiding collision with street fixtures, streams of people and other rickshaws. What is striking is the astute navigational sense of the rickshaw drivers, which is quite typical of the Banarasi way of life.

Rickshaw graphics are an interesting dimension of the popular culture of Banaras. The imagery is often taken from religious art but presented with kitsch. Common motifs are elephants, horses, birds, fish and often a pair of eyes.

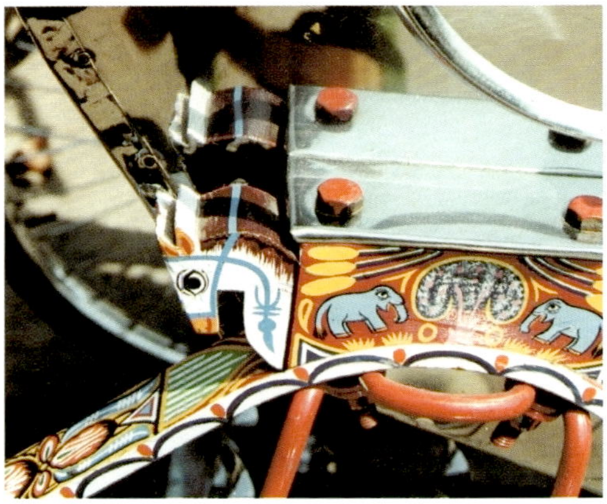

Rickshaw owners personalize their vehicles in their own ways, by pasting an image of a favourite deity or inscribing the names of their family members on it. They add little accessories to it like electric lights, fancy mirrors or hang charms like garlands of lemons and chillies that are meant to ward off the evil eye. It is clear that they love their vehicles and groom it like proud parents would a child. On a lazy afternoon, one might spot several rickshaws parked on one end of Asi Ghat, by the banks of the Ganga, being bathed and polished for hours.

THE E-RICKSHAW

The E-rickshaw is a culturally reflective artifact that allows people to interact not with a computer, but with the rickshaw itself.

When current forms of computing consisting of keyboard, mouse and TV display disappear, it can assume the forms of walls, tables, furniture, clothing, in the forms of preceding technologies which are already part of people's social fabric and awareness.

In this installation the form of a computer disappears and reappears as a popular cultural icon of Banaras, the rickshaw. The rickshaw travels through the artscapes and landscapes of Banaras. The e-rickshaw allows users to interact with rickshaw accessories to retrieve video images showing the rickshaw in Banaras, its streets, the geometry, and the love of the driver for his vehicle. The rickshaw stories on the streets of Banaras can be explored by steering the handle of a rickshaw.

The combination of the rickshaw and info-kiosk may create a new genre of community walk-up kiosks. The easy access, the disappearance of the keyboard, and the walk-up nature of the kiosk allow cultural objects such as a rickshaw to become a community access tool.

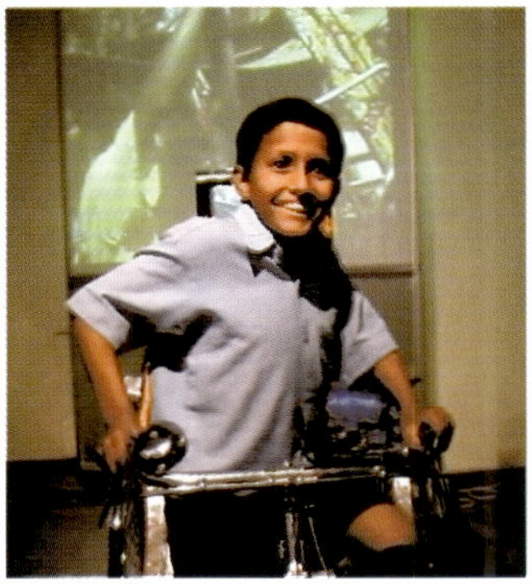

The Cycle Jhalla Video Installation

The music of the five videos in this installation was based on the musical structure of the "jhalla". Jhalla is a part of classical raga performance in which the musician underscores the rhythm strings of a stringed instrument, such as a sitar. Five compositions of jhalla formed the bases of the Cycle Jhalla videos.

The raga selected for the Cycle Jhalla compositions is *Raga Malkauns. Raga Malkauns* is a pentatonic raga with the notes *Sa, Ga, Ma, Dha, Ni,* (roughly C, Eb, F, Ab, Bb, in a key of C.

The mantra of Shiva 'Na' 'Ma' 'Shi' 'Va' 'Ya', is composed of five syllables. Shiva as a personification of space, i.e., five directions, is known as Sada Shiva. The association of the number five provided the structure for the Cycle Jhalla compositions, and the compositions themselves were created in a rhythmic cycle of ten beats divided (5,5).

Composition[1] THE JHALLA

This video captures the visual imagery of the cycle rickshaw through the streetscapes of Banaras.

Composition^2 JOURNEY

This video presents an adventurous journey from the passengers' point of view as the rickshaw meanders through the narrow lanes of Banaras.

Composition^3 CHAOS

This video captures the chaos and cacophony at "Gadaulia Chowk", Banaras' busiest traffic intersection.

This video treats the rickshaw as a work of art and captures its movement, geometry and form.

Composition^{5} LOVE

The intimate bond between the rickshawallah and his vehicle.
This video portrays a poetic sequence of the rickshawallah grooming his rickshaw by the Ganga.
The dust and the din of the day is washed away by the cool and purifying waters of the Ganga.

MUSICAL WHEEL

One can strike a chord with the musical-scape of the city by plucking the spokes of the musical wheel.

By combining properties of one physical media with another, through embedded computation, users can explore physical morphing. Here the cycle wheel is transformed into musical instruments, the sitar and tabla, resonating *Raga Malkauns.*

Associated with each spoke is a musical note, drum beat, musical or rythmic phrases, and plucking the rickshaw spoke allows people to explore sitar and tabla sounds and to collaboratively produce music.

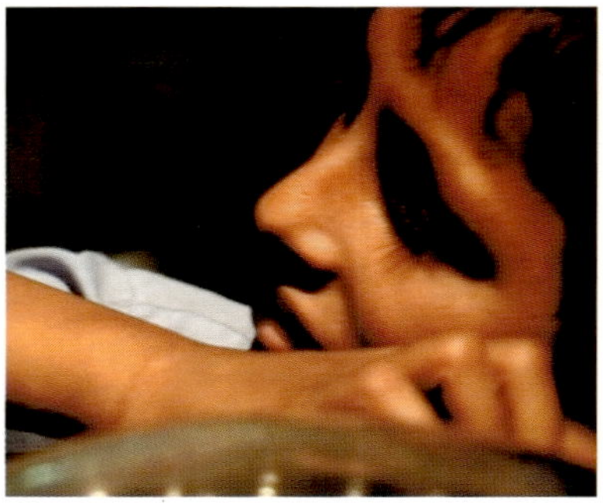

The circular form of the musical wheel allows many people to collaborate and communicate with each other, i.e. see the spokes, as well as each other's eyes and hands. Hence this musical wheel is a multi-person collaborative instrument.

PHYSICAL VIRTUAL PORTAL

In this installation, a spinning cycle wheel suggests the volume of traffic in Gadaulia Chowk, Banaras' busiest intersection. The wheel spins faster when the junction is engulfed in traffic jams, and slow when traffic is flowing.

So by looking at the spinning wheel, instead of a display screen, one can deduce the traffic in Gadaulia Chowk. Ordinary physical objects are transformed into a display screen.

Such a simple idea of creating physical displays can allow people in villages to avoid the LCD as a mode of display, and to explore alternate forms of physical displays through transformable physical displays, which illustrate changes in physical states.

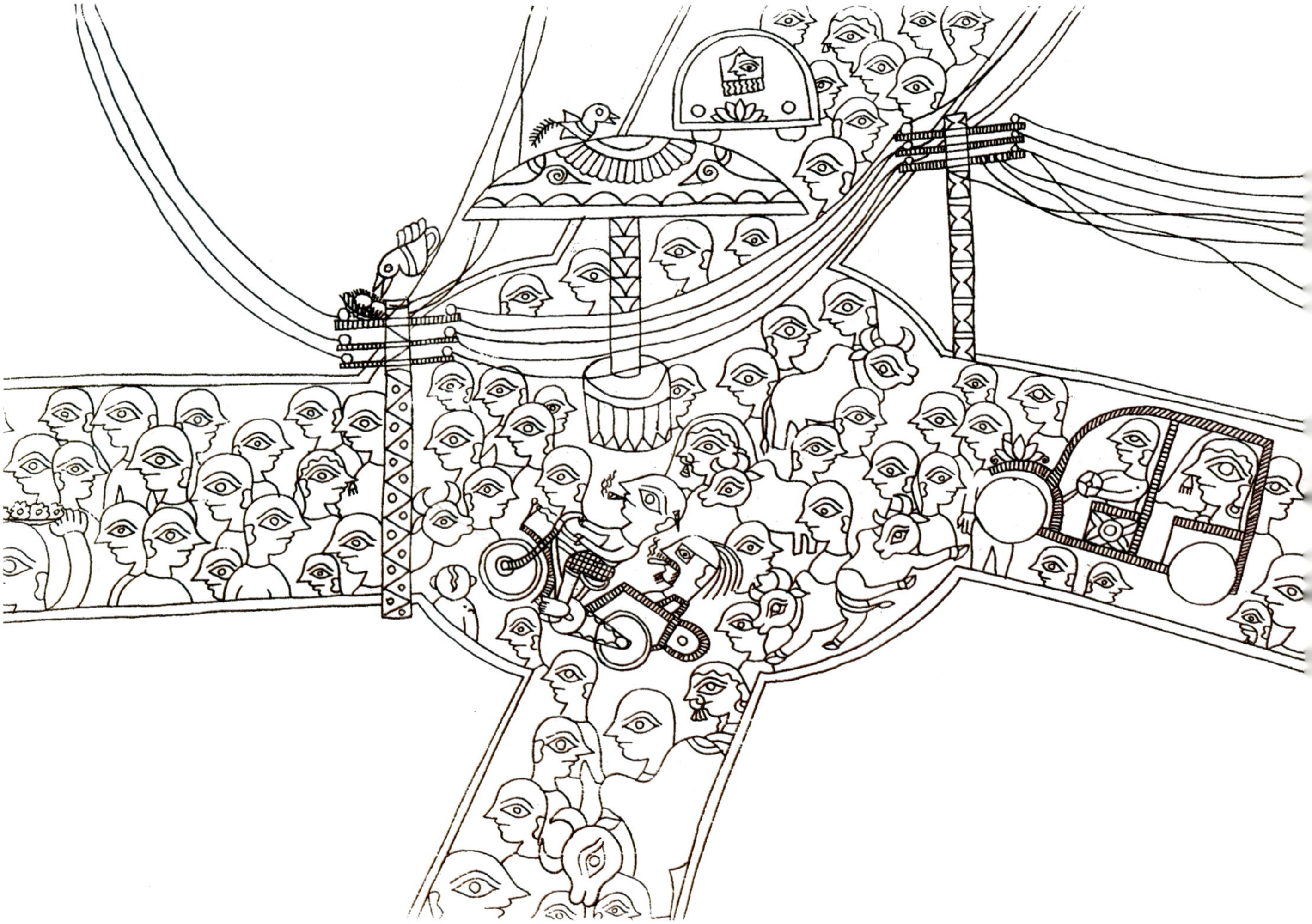

Gadaulia Chowk, Banaras

If one were to sum up the entire gamut of Varanasi culture in one or two words, they would be Mauj and Masti. . . . The former epitomizes all that goes by the generic terms, enjoyment, conviviality, festivity, jollity, gaiety, and other similar ideas, while Masti envisages contentment, serenity, placidity, tranquility, exhilaration, geniality, buoyancy, self-esteem, heartiness, and even recklessness and wayward up buoyancy.

Kuber Nath Sukul, Varanasi Down the Ages: 1974: 325

Mauj Masti

Since ancient times, Banaras has been recognized to have its distinct individuality. Just like the faithscape of the city, even the Banarasis have evolved an attitude and a philosophy of life quite different from anywhere else. The people of Banaras follow their own "Banarasi" way of life, a style of living, which defies rational explanation. In Banaras it is said that bathing, grooming, and eating... if these three are taken care of, then a man is leading a perfect life! Banaras has this special magnetism in its environment, attitude and way of life.

The spiritual exaltation of the Vedic lore trickled down into a carefree day-to-day life of a Banarasi. The typical Banarasi is unaffected by adversities because, he believes that Lord Shiva and Goddess Annapurna have endowed him with special courage and strength to cope with the calamities of existence. Why weep when ultimate bliss is reassured in Kashi. This faith has inspired the people to live with contentment and to ultimately surrender their bodies in the city of Shiva. The people of Banaras are famous for living in delight (mauj) and gay abandon. They exude a certain zest and passion for life which is described as Banarasipan. Their way of life is carefree and based on simplicity, contentment, and a love and addiction for some things typically

Banarasi, such as chewing a mouthful of *paan,* drinking rose-scented *thandai,* taking *bhang* or indulging in certain activities, such as bathing, sauntering by the ghats, wrestling or going to musical gatherings. Among their many likes, Banarasis specially love cleanliness of the body and clothes. They have a culture of frequent washing of garments in the water of the Ganga. This is known as Safa-pani. From the humble boatman to the lofty aristocrat, they are all seen by the riverbank with their gamchas - a hand-spun towel that serves both as a bathing garment, and a scarf or multipurpose wrap. It is said that the gamcha is sometimes seen as a symbol of Banarasi culture.

The love for physical fitness in the Banarasi idiom is equally enthralling. It is said that out of a 100 Banarasis that one encounters, 99 belong to the traditional akhara or gymnasium where young men undergo a traditional regimen of body building. Their love for dressing and adornment is reflected in their *paan*-stained mouths, use of a variety of fragrances or attars, each for a different season and time of the day, and hand-woven Banarasi silks with which women and men adorn themselves. Whether rich or poor the Banarasis live with a strong sense of pride. It is well acknowledged that each person considers himself to be a king. Large hearted and accommodating, the Banarasis revel in a joke or two at their expense. The Kashika, the colloquial language of Banaras, is very amenable to double entendres and multiple meanings. These features have given Banarasis a very special character of their own. The Banarasis call it Mauj Masti, living and flowing on a wave of intoxication arising from sheer enjoyment of life. Despite the diversity of caste, religion, sect and nationality, all have become followers of this creed.

THE BANARASI PAAN

The culture of *paan* has been refined over generations to such a degree that all across Banaras each and every paan has a distinct identity.

It is a daily ritual to clean the paan with water, wipe it with cloth after which it is put back into water to retain its freshness. The spoilt parts of the leaf are trimmed. The leaf slowly matures from a green to an off white colour. To this leaf is added a small amount of betel lime, some betel gum or *katha* and a piece of betel nut. The *katha* is such that local connoisseurs will tell you, whether it was made by Bansi, Dwarka or Babunandan, or if it was made in Asi, or somewhere else. The flavour is distinct from place to place within Banaras.

"We always make sure that anyone who eats the paan we make, walks out feeling like they've eaten something really special," says a famous paanwallah at Gadaulia Chowk.

According to a local connoisseur, "Once the paan has been kept in the mouth, it is not the Banarasi way to chew it, or spit it out, rather, we just keep it in the mouth for a long time!...Banarasis don't put fifty spices in their *paan.* They will keep it in their mouth for hours and tell you "Look this *paan* is four days old! only its juice is meant to trickle down your throat!"

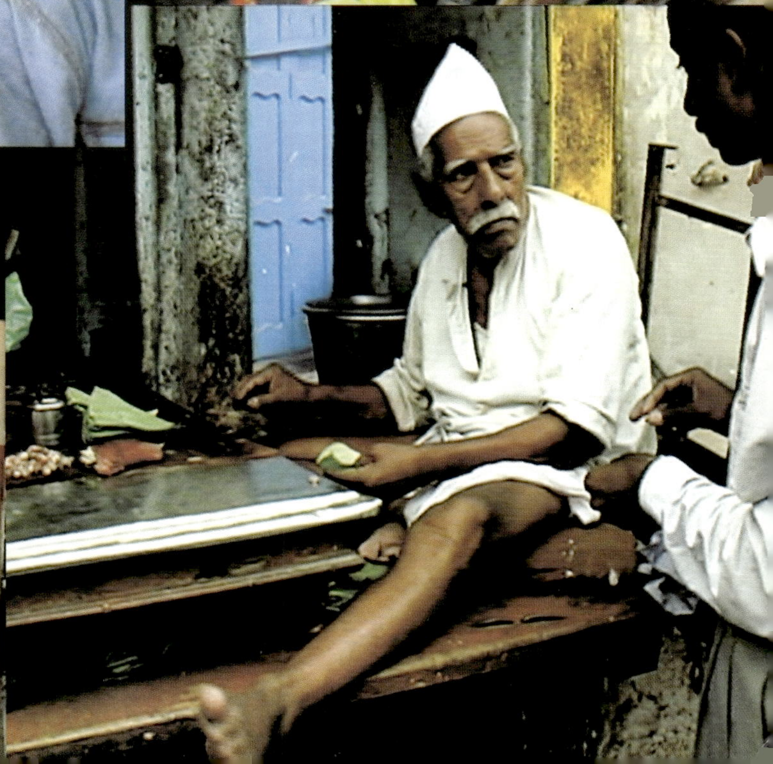

INTOXICATION & CELEBRATION

The Banarasis on Mauj and Masti

- excerpts from the video script, "The Art of Living"

Being content with the least, delighting in the smallest of pleasures... this is the vision of life here. It is not a doctrine or religion, it is a style of life or a way of life. This has been the basis of life in Banaras since ancient times.

A dialogue between *Professor Anand Krishna (AK), Dr. Bhanushankar Mehta (BM), Sh. Shashank Singh (SS), Sh. Mukund Lal (ML) and Sh. Poorna Chand (PC).*

ANAND KRISHNA (video clip)

"It is said that Kashi is really an extraordinary place.
And the most important thing is that Kashi is the creation of Lord Shankar, his very own."

"It is said that 'Kashi is beyond the three worlds.'... meaning...that the Banarasis had created a world of their own, that set them apart from every other place." -(AK)

"Banaras had this special magnetism, in its environment, its attitude, and its way of life." - (SS)

"Here, people used to get up very early and go to the Ganga to bathe.The Banarasi man, loves to wrestle and sport, he would joyfully die for Banaras. Jaishankar Prasadji has called them, ' The lion spirited ones.' They used to live with pride and honour." - (BM)

"There was one very important thing in their lives, cleanliness." - (AK)

"It is known as *saapha paani*." - (BM)

"It basically means that even if you have a clean cloth, you want to wash it again!" - (AK)

"Banarasis wash their *gamchas* (towels) in the Ganga, then leave it to dry, wrap around another *gamcha* and bathe. The *gamcha* is like the flag of Banaras... an identity. It's a multipurpose cloth." - (BM)

MUKUNDA LAL (video clip)

"In Banaras it is said that bathing, grooming, and eating.... if these three are taken care of, then a man is leading a perfect life." - (ML)

"There is one thing I want to tell you, particularly, a certain word is used here, that is 'Divya'. Divya means divine. A divine bath, divine siesta or a divine meal...blissful and full of joy." - (BM)

"People say that Banarasis spend half their time in *paan* shops, (*paan* is a special delicacy prepared with betel leaf, nuts and condiments.)...half their lives infact." - (ML)

"The spoken language of Banaras is called Kashika...it is basically an indirect, symbolic language...with up to three or four connotations in any sentence.The phrase "Khaa ke Jao" could be an invitation to have a *paan*, or if you want to insult someone, it could also mean asking the person to go to hell!" - (BM)

BHANUSHANKAR MEHTA (video clip)

"The word Banaras, in popular parlance means essence of life . You'll find every kind of flavour, taste, and fragrance, here..." - (PC)

"Milk and jalebis...jalebis are made in many places but no one makes them like they are made here...A typical Banarasi has his breakfast, and then wants to rest...when he wakes up it's already noon. There's no mention of going to work yet...it's already time for lunch...Then he has some lunch,and of course one needs a little nap after a meal...he has his afternoon siesta." - (BM)

"The people are very easy-going, they delight in the simple joys of existence. You could never tell if they are heavily in debt, had other worries... But when it came to living the good life, they lived without cares." - (AK)

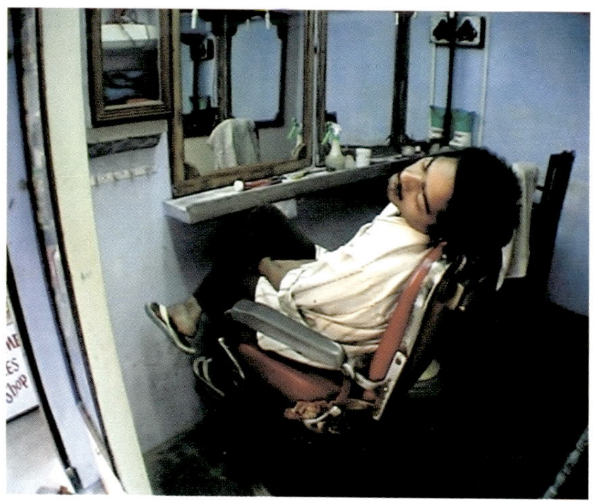

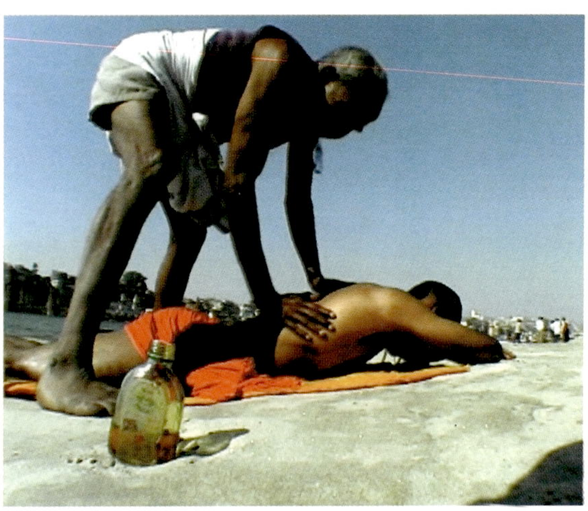

Banaras is suffused with the essence of the Ganga. The cool breeze along the banks creates a pleasant atmosphere of tranquility providing space for several leisure activities. People enjoy the beauty of the river by walking along the banks, indulging in water sports, going for a boat ride or merely resting by the ghats.

SHASHANKA SINGH (video clip)

"Living a carefree life, relishing it, was important to the Banarasi, and this way of living is sadly, coming to an end...." - (BM)

"There are two important factors, one is that this is a city of pilgrimage, second is that it is a city with different trades, like manufacturing of sarees.In this trade you have a lot of time to yourself. If there are no pilgrims,then the trader is idle..." - (AK)

"Eight o' clock at night, the Banarasi ventures out, and business begins. In the art of making sarees, jewellery...in each of their crafts they had a unique style...If a single saree sold for a hundred odd rupees, that meant a commission of just ten rupees for him, enough for a month's holiday." - (BM)

"If he heard strains of good music from somewhere, he'd make his way to it. If he liked the performance,then the musician received heartfelt appreciation with cries of 'Wah! Wah!'. In terms of rewarding people, the Banarasi was more than generous. Even if he had only one rupee in his pocket and that was all he had to eat and drink...if someone made him happy, then he'd reward them with it, saying 'go enjoy yourself'..So what if it meant no meals the next day." - (BM)

"Money was not a major thing, and this wasn't about exhibiting your wealth. This lifestyle was about understanding and recognizing the value of it in terms of a participative society." - (AK)

"They could be described as *man ke raja*, meaning, kings in their own right" - (SS)

"No law of the world can run this place. It is said that, this is the only city where there is no kingdom,there are only kings. People keep saying, "Kaa Raja...", addressing each other as kings, even though they possessed nothing." - (PC)

"Being content with the least, delighting in the smallest of pleasures..this is the vision of life here. It is not a doctrine or religion, it is a style of life or a way of life. This has been the basis of life in Banaras since ancient times." - (BM)

PURNA CHANDRA (video clip)

"Whatever the Lord gives you, be it just a tiny morsel of food, and Ganga water, rejoice in it, but never leave Kashi for this is the court of Lord Vishvanath." - (PC)

E-EGG

The E-egg is a multidimensional cultural artifact. Its form is derived from the form of *Brahmanda,* or the cosmic egg described in the Vedas as well as in the form of the universe described by modern physicists. The egg is also the form naturally created when the hands assume a cupped position. In contrast to rectilinear, inorganic objects characteristic of computer delivery devices, the e-egg responds to the mythical dimensions as well as the physical dimensions of the body.

Engravings on the e-egg demarcate zones of Mauj Masti in Banaras, and touching them allows people to play back images of happiness and relaxation in the streets of Banaras. The engravings create a rich textural space, and one can recognize the diverse streets of Banaras by rubbing the hands on the e-egg with one's eyes closed. The e-egg forces designers to explore texture as a useful, haptic input in communicating "state" changes.

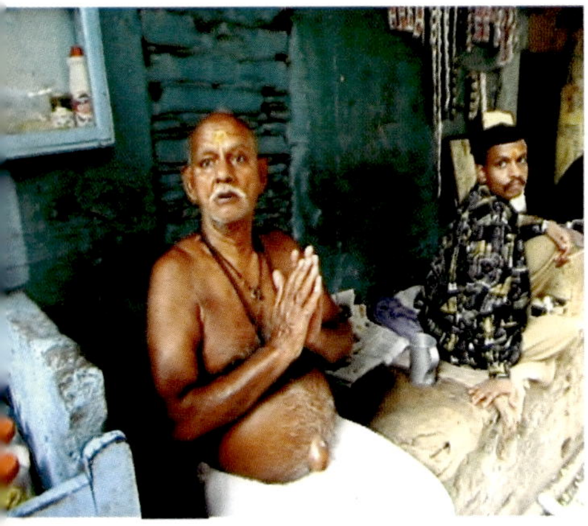

Mauj Masti Display

The narrow zigzagging lanes and bazaars of Banaras celebrate every form of sense perceptions—sight, sound, touch, fragrance, and intoxicants. The kaleidoscopic display of the "Mauj Masti" traps the user into the Banarasi's world of "Samsara".

The immersion of the user need not only occur within the boundaries of small rectangular display screens, but rather in architectonic space. This brings up the role of scale of the display and relationship of the display to the body. It also brings the role of the periphery. Traditional computing displays allow people to focus on "centres", literally holes in the wall, yet spatial and visual perception occurs through the periphery. By embedding display technology into physical active wall surfaces, people could engage with computing content through the periphery.

TILTY TABLE

We re-question the form of a modern workstation and its underlying assumptions. The substrate of the form of the modern computing display and interface is based on a 30-year-old form of mouse-keyboard-display-and-television monitor based learning system. While this form has spawned rich genres of presentations, it has created a separation between people's hands and eyes.

The tilty table display and interface allows users to browse through a large map of Banaras fusing display and interface. Tilting the display causes the image of the map to scroll in the direction of the tilt as though the image was subject to the forces of gravity.

Tilty Table with P V Shopping

By navigating the tilty table with images of the narrow lanes of Banaras, the cursor representing the shopper can enter the shops to trigger the play back of video imagery, showing the intense process of trading in Banaras' streets.

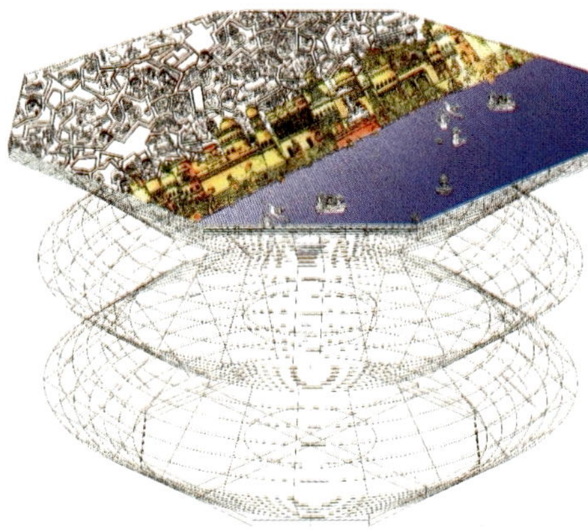

Shiva

The holy family in Mount Kailash.
Pahari Style. Contemporary.

The city of Kashi derives its sanctity from its intimate association with Lord Shiva, who is one of the most formidable personifications in the Hindu pantheon. The early history of Shiva describes his ancient embodiment as that of an ascetic mountain god with his abode in the snowy peaks of Mount Kailash in the northern Himalaya. When he married Paravati and assumed the role of a householder, he needed a home in the city. His relocation to the city of Kashi is a major episode in mythology. It is said that from all the places on the earth, Shiva chose Kashi as his home but could not live there until he won over the city from Divodasa, the king who once ruled there. With the mass exodus that followed, the ruling king and his subjects vacated the city.

Shiva and Paravati and their family come down from the mountains.
Pahari style, Kangra. 18th century.

Shiva moved there with his entourage. Since then Kashi is regarded as Shiva's earthly home where he manifests himself in his multiple forms ruling over Kashi with his queen, Annapurna Bhavani. Annapurna (literally, Abundant with Food) is the gracious lady who provides food to one and all. Together, Shiva and Annapurna fulfill the most basic needs of sacred life. Annapurna provides food for nourishment, while Shiva grants liberation.

Linga of Light

Kashi is regarded as the eternal dwelling place of Shiva, where he resides in his multiple personifications. It is believed that Kashi came into existence when Lord Shiva manifested there as a pillar of light, or *Jyotirlinga*, which in Hindu mythology is a symbol of the central axis of the universe.

At the time of creation a cosmic explosion of light appeared and that column of light blazed up and split the earth. The circumference of the *Jyotirlinga* covered the entire landmass of Kashi.

A story from the corpus of Shiva myths describes the emergence of the *Jyotirlinga* in Kashi. Brahma, the creator, Vishnu, the preserver were arguing about the supremacy of one over the other. They called upon the Vedas to settle the dispute.

The Vedas proclaimed that neither of them were supreme, but it is Shiva who is the supreme Lord. The two gods stood in awe as a massive column split the earth and blazed up to the highest point visible in the sky to pierce the heavens. Astounded, Brahma and Vishnu set out to determine the extent of the pillar of light. Vishnu leaped as a boar to the netherworld, while Brahma mounted his goose and flew to heaven. But even after a thousand years they could not find either the bottom or the top of the Linga of Light. They returned to the starting point and Shiva revealed himself from the fiery Linga in a "partial" body form. After this, Shiva bestowed a boon that this infinite Linga of Light would become so small that people

The Cosmic form of Shiva with a halo of light.
Pahari style. Contemporary.

Shiva receiving alms from goddess Annapurna. *Bhasholi style. Contemporary.*

would be able to worship it. All the Shiva lingas in Kashi are regarded to be refractions of this light. The Vishvanatha temple, as it stands today, is said to house the primal *Jyotirlinga*.

It is not easy to characterize Shiva's personality, for his personification has developed through accretion from a multitude of elements traceable to Vedic, tantric, and popular folk cults. Many elements of Shiva's iconography reflect the assimilation of primal and possibly, non-Aryan traits. His pronounced ascetic features, such as the matted lock of hair, ornaments of skulls and snakes are traceable to the primitive layers of early Indian civilization. Alongside this, there is an overlay of interpretations offered by the sophisticated layers of Hindu society. It has been widely accepted by scholars that in the early phase of history, Shiva was an ascetic god living in the Kailash mountains. Some time, around the fourth century AD, in the epic period, when the ideal of the divine couple was held in high esteem, his marriage to Paravati became an essential feature in his mythology. Thereupon, Shiva's ascetic persona acquired another identity. He was to play a more humanised role of a householder, a husband to goddess Paravati, and father two sons. By the mediaeval period both these identities—of ascetic and householder *(yogi cum bhogi)*—get merged, and Shiva emerges as an all inclusive god, playing dual or even multiple roles. Both feared and loved, his personality assimilates contradictions in a singular personification. Shiva's early history as an ascetic defies all the norms of Brahmanical orthodoxy—purity, auspiciousness, custom, morality founded on the codes of *dharma,* lineage or social status. In this aspect Shiva is an outisder, the "other" far removed from the norm, living in the margins of society, contradicting every defining category of Hindu *dharma.* As the most perfect of all yogis, Shiva appears as a fierce wanderer on the burning grounds of Kashi, with ash-smeared body rapt in deep meditation. At the same time, when the ascetic god transforms into a beautiful husband, his ash-smeared body is anointed with fragrant pungents, and he plays the role of an indulgent husband enjoying domestic bliss with his wife, Annapurna Bhavani and his two sons, Ganesha and Kartikeya.

Rama and Lakshmana pay homage to Shiva ard Paravati
Pahari style. Kangra. 18th century.

Shiva as Bhairava (detail).
Folk style, Rajasthan. 20th century.

In the Puranas, Shiva's enigmatic personality is a source of wonder to all.

He is not an ascetic, for how can one who carries a weapon be an ascetic?
He is not a householder, for he lives in the cremation ground.
He is not a celibate student, for he has a wife. And he cannot be a forest-dweller, for he is drunk with the conceit of his lordship.
He is not a brahmin, for the Vedas do not know him as one. Since he carries a spear and a trident, he might be a kshatriya, but he is not. Since he delights in the destruction of the world, he cannot be a kshatriya, who protects the world from harm.
And how can he a vaishya, for he never has any wealth?
He is not even a shudra, for he wears the snake as a sacred thread. So he is beyond the castes (varna)

Ardhanarishvara (detail)
Bhasholi style, 19th century.

and the stages of life (ashrama). *Everything is known by its original source* (prakriti), *but Shiva the Immovable has no original source.*
He is not a man, because half his body is female. And yet he is not a woman, because he has a beard. He is not even a eunuch, because his phallus (linga) *is worshipped.*
He is not a boy, for he is great in years, that fearsome one, and he is proclaimed in the world as beginningless and ageless. How can he be young when he is so ancient? And yet he is not old, for he is without old age and death.

Skanda Purana(Kashi Khanda)Chapter 87.28-37 cited in Diana L Eck, City of Light, 1983:100

Shiva as Bhairava.
Folk style, Rajasthan.
20th century.

Kashi is synonymous with Lord Shiva where he resides in his multiple personifications. In his androgynous form Shiva manifests as the undivided male and female principles in one body.

As Mahayogi, he represents the perfection of austerity, penance, and equilibrium of the spirit.
As Bhairava, he is the active principle of destruction; as Mahakala, he is the divinity of Supreme Time.

As Mrityunjaya, he is the death conquering divinity who heals the body and grants immortality; wedded to Paravati, he is a domesticated husband; and as Shankar and Bholenatha, he is the auspicious one who bestows grace to all.

And, finally as Sadashiva, the Five-Faced one he rules over all aspects of creation. Shiva is a complete god whose personality gathers together and harmonises all the paradoxes and oppositions of existence.

Shiva as Mrityunjaya, the death conquering deity.
Pahari style, Kangra.
c.19th century.

The divine couple,
Shiva and Paravati as Bhairava and Bhairavi seated on a lotus pedestal.
Pahari style, Kangra. Late 20th century.

Sadashiva with Paravati and Nandi.
Bhasholi style, c. Late 19th century

SADASHIVA

Shiva as Sadashiva, the five-faced one, is the eternal principle. As Sadashiva, the Eternal one, Shiva is represented as five-faced. Of the five faces, four faces, face the four cardinal directions. In this aspect, Shiva symbolizes all aspects of creation and is a progenitor of the five orders of creation.

The face of Shiva, pearly white, that looks up is named Ishan, The Lord or the Ruler. Ishan is all omniscient, the master of all knowledge and forms of learning and presides over the element, air.

Sadashiva icon carved on the linga at Omkareshvara Temple, Banaras

The eastern face of Shiva, yellow in colour, is called Tatpurusha, the supreme one. This aspect represents that which is enjoyed, that is the Prakriti or material nature and presides over the element, earth.

The southern face of Shiva is named Aghora. It is dark blue or of blue-black hue, and presides over the element, ether. Aghora represents the principles of intellect or the law of eternal dharma.

The western face of Shiva, Vamadeva is red. He presides over the awareness of ego-sense and the element, fire.

The northern face of Shiva, Sadyojata is white. This aspect of Shiva symbolizes the mind and the faculty of discrimination and presides over the element, water.

As the ruler of the five directions of space, of the five elements, of five senses, of all that is ruled by the five acts of the cosmos: creation, preservation, withdrawal, veiling and bestowal of grace, Shiva represents the All, as Sadashiva.

Umapathy explains the iconometry and symbolism of the five-faced Shiva. (video clip).

Alarmel Valli performing "An offering to Shiva," *Om Namah Shivaya* in Bharatnatyam sty e. (video clip)

Guru Kelucharan Mahapatra performing a piece on "Panchmukhi Shiva" in Odissi style. (video clip)

Sadashiva (detail) Pahari style, contemporary.

Kalanidhi Narayan expressing through abhinaya the "Navrasas of Shiva" in Bharatnatyam style. (video clip)

Priyadarshini Govind expressing the love play of Shiva and Paravati based on "Kumarsambhava" by Kalidasa, in Bharatnatyam style. (video clip)

Shiva and Paravati and Ganga issuing from Shiva's locks Kangra style, 19th century.

The adorning of icons and the joining of icons can evolve gestures and composite forms that are meaningful in cultural contexts. The joining of the Linga (the male form) and the Yoni (the female form) creates a composite form that allows people to access notions of male-female unity.

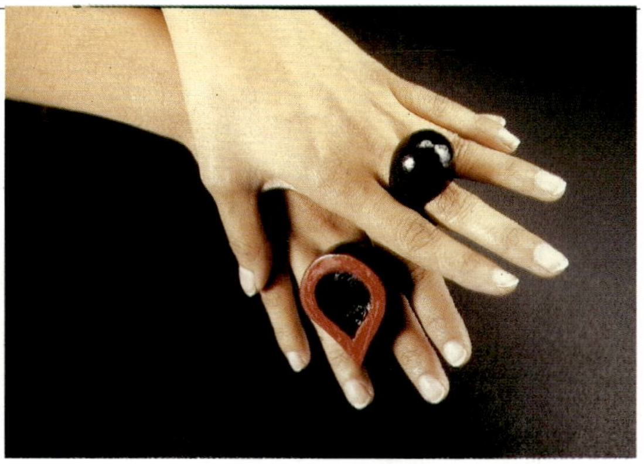

Icons can transform their appearance physically, illustrating changes in state. The opening of this icon box completes t symbol of the heave flow of the Ganga fr Shiva's matted locks.

Tactile Icons

The world of Indian arts speaks about the interrelationship among the visual, plastic and performing arts. That which can be seen can also be felt. In the installation, the 14 emblems of Shiva's yogic form are augmented with radio tags. Users hold an icon and touch a display screen to retrieve the image of a dancer explaining the inner meaning of the symbols of Shiva, such as his wisdom eye, crescent moon, his matted locks, serpent garland, tiger skin, etc.

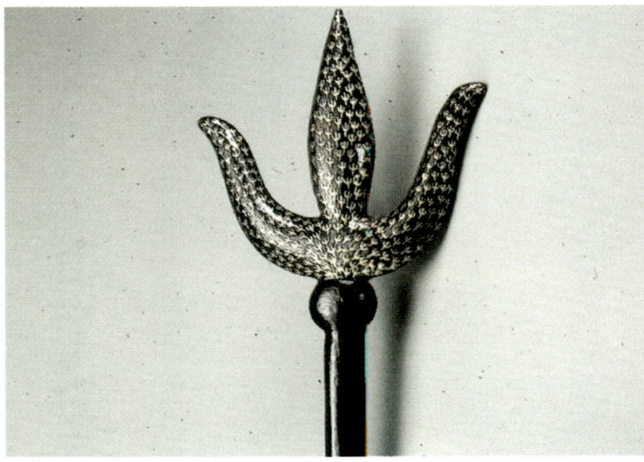

Priyadarshini Govind depicting the iconography of Shiva through hand gestures and shadows in Bharatnatyam style.(video clip)

E-Shiva Egg

The forms created by human hands can shape delivery devices. Just as a potter's thumb shapes the radius of the pot, we can design interfaces that respond to the forms of the hands. In doing so, we move from touching impersonal "black and beige" boxes to personalized forms and sensuous materials, and eventually from inorganic materials to earth friendly materials.

Out of the many positions possible in the human hand, our interactions with computing interfaces have been reduced to button-pushing. How do we restore the dimensions of gesture in the design of devices?

Forms suggest our connection to larger dimensions. The origins of ritual gesture suggest this, and through carefully positioned figure positions of the hands, gesture evokes inner intelligence states. Since modern man spends a major portion of time interacting with devices, could we not explore a new set of forms that provoke inner intelligence states?

Below
Initial forms of computing interface and work stations have been based on "black and beige" forms. Yet our hands produce curved shapes and forms. Can new designs incorporate texture, and earth friendly forms?

"The etymology of the word "lingam" is from the Sanskrit root, *lina*, meaning, to dissolve or merge. Thus, the lingam symbol of Shiva, represents that primal essence which absorbs the universe within itself.

The linga embodies cosmic space,
the mighty earth is its throne,
from the earth to the heavens
the linga is thus the abode of all Gods,

The eminent scientist of the 20th century, Albert Einstein, also proved that space is curved...Is not the curve of space like the curve of the lingam? When you see a linga it resembles the primal form of a cosmic egg."

- Mahant Ram Shankar Tripathi (video clip)

E-LINGA

The E-linga installation explores info-kiosks made out of organic materials, eg., the fired earth, and suggests how displays can be incorporated in natural forms evolved by rural communities.

Visualization of the Forest of Linga myth. Banaras is also known as the forest of lingas. Millions of lingas in Banaras mirror the original "Linga of Light" myth. In this visualization, based on the form of Shiva as Vastospati, the Lord of the ordered cosmos, Linga computers allow people to access the content of Shiva's multiple forms.

Jala-abhisheka at Tarakeshvara Temple, Manikarnika ghat

Meaning of Linga

At Kashi, Shiva is worshipped in his iconic as well as his aniconic symbol, the Linga (literally "sign" or "emblem"). The most universal representation of Shiva is the Linga. The Linga is the most sacred object of adoration. It is considered more sacred than the anthropomorphic image. While the anthropomorphic image is the gross body of God, the Linga is said to be the subtle *nishkala*, aspect of Shiva, a symbol without parts, a complete whole, wherein Shiva resides eternally. The Linga is a phallic-shaped vertical stone, pointing towards the heavens. The upright stone is self-existing containing Shiva's potential energy in seed form. The Linga is embedded in a symbolic container, a yoni pedestal or *bhaga*, representing the female principle, divined as goddess Paravati. The sanctum sanctorum of every Shiva temple in Banaras houses a stone Linga. The primal Lingas are self-manifested stones or natural pebbles shaped by the flow of the river, found in the bed of the Narmada or hilly tracts in the Himalaya. They have certain natural markings, which makes them distinct. They are called Bana Lingas. There are some that are handcrafted adhering to the rules of the aesthetic canon. It is held that all the different types of Shiva Lingas installed in Banaras are sparks of the primal Linga of Light that shone with searing glory at the beginning of creation.

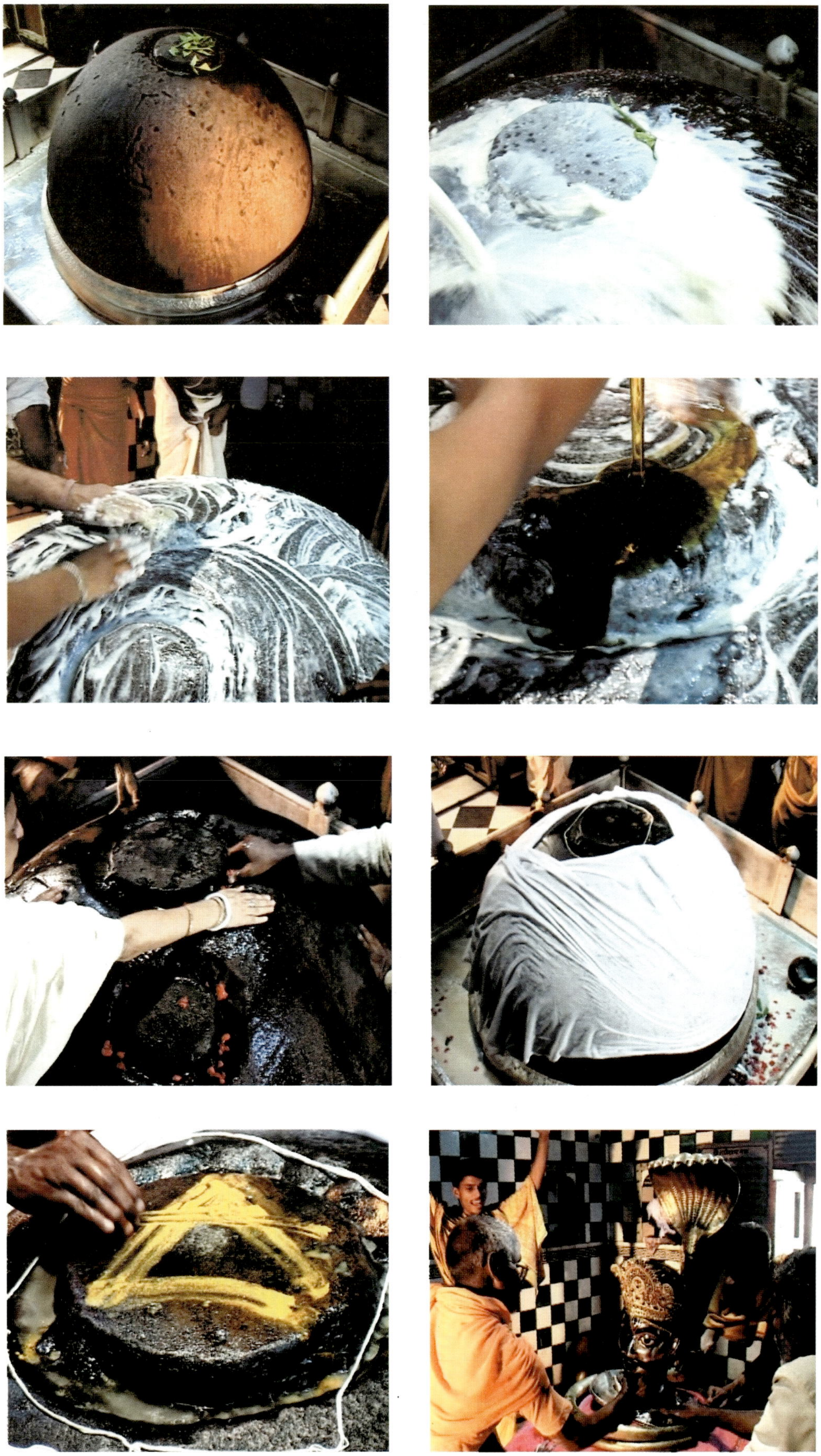

Abhishekha at Tilabhandeshvara Temple, Banaras (vedio clip)

Worship of Shiva

The rituals of Abhishekha illustrates traditional forms of "interaction design". The ritual involves integration of body, materials and symbol. People interact with forms of Shiva with complete engagement of the overall body. The symbolic annointment of the linga with various natural materials, eg., five sweets, flowers, ritual ingredients illustrates a highly sophisticated form of traditional interaction design and multi-media. This involves all senses, colour, sound and texture, and the overall engagement of the body in relation to the symbol.

The Linga is worshipped with an innumerable variety of liquids. It is said that Shiva is pleased with *jaladhara*, a constant flow of water from a ritual pot, the base of which is perforated at the centre. The pot is placed or hung above the Shiva Linga. The Linga is anointed with pure water, milk, honey, buttermilk, herbs, clarified butter and holy ash to the chant of the famous Rudra Shiva mantra, hymns from the Vedas or his five-syllabled mantra. After the ablution, the Linga is propitiated with Bilva leaves (*Aegle marmelos*), flowers, garlands, incense, and waving of lamps and offering of holy food.

He is not an ascetic, for how can one

He is not a householder, for he lives

who carries a weapon be an ascetic?

in the cremation ground.

Sacred Geography

The most sacred part of the city is the crescent-shaped river-front with its stepped embankment (ghats) that lead to the river. Stretching from Asi in the south to the Adi Keshava in the north, extending to three miles, there are 84 ghats which are lined with stone terraces, Linga images, shrines, and *ashrams.* Many of them mark important places of pilgrimage. These ghats are essentially perceived as a faithscape, an amphitheatre of collective memories that recall the mythical world of gods and goddesses, and divine events. The sacred stories are imprinted on the ghats and run as a subtext. The ghats are one of the most spectacular altars to the Hindu faith. From dawn to dusk, the ghats teem with sacred activity all the year around where pilgrims and devotees perform ablutions and prayers, daily and seasonal rituals, take sin-cleansing holy dips and perform the last "death" rites for kith and kin. The ghats derive their significance not merely from the beauty of their architecture, but through their place-specifc myths and stories of divine enactments of the gods that took place in primal times. Each ghat is linked with a sacred happening and is touched by the supernatural forces of the cosmos. It is on the ghats that one encounters the overlayering of religious symbols that have accrued through Banaras' ancient history traceable to 7000 BC.

The Varuna and Asi are the two rivers set by the gods. Between them is the holy land and there is none more excellent on earth.

—Padma Purana cited in Diana L Eck, City of Light, 1993: 26.

360° SWIVEL DISPLAY

When computation in its current form of display keyboard-mouse disappears and enters the physical world, the laws of gravity apply. Hence its objects understand their position, their orientation, and displays "understand" tilt and turn and which side is up and down. This presents a rich space of physical computing, where the position of the display is an input to the retrieval of content.

We always wondered what lies beyond the edge of a display screen. The 360° Display browser allows us to explore spaces beyond the rigid rectangles of display.

One can swivel the display to explore the panoramic view of Banaras' river and temple-spired skyline. The browser presents the user with an experience of being situated in the middle of the Ganga river and exploring the panoramic view of the river.

Indeed because of the significance of the ghats, the area stretching between the two rivers Varuna in the south and Asi in the north is considered to be the most sacred tract of land on earth. The two rivers that embrace the river-front are compared to a woman whose two arms cradled the ghats. Located on the southern tip of the river-front, the Asi ghat is one of the oldest ghats. The Sanskrit word, Asi means a sharp sword. In the *Skanda Purana* (30. 18), it is said that the river Asi, like a sword, rents asunder the evil intentions of impure beings. The significance of Asi is enhanced because of the location of Sangameshvara, the Lord of the confluence of the two rivers in a small shrine where the plaque reads "all the *tirthas* that girdle the earth are not equal to a sixteenth part of the Asi Sangam."

To the north of the Asi ghat lies the celebrated Lolarka Kunda, one of the 14 major shrines dedicated to the sun. At daybreak, the cluster of lingas most ardently revered here are the ones that are established under the far-spreading pipal (*Ficus Religiosa*) tree. Walking along Asi, towards the south, lies Tulsi ghat, of fairly recent orign.

Opposite page
Kadamba tree-worship at Asi ghat during the month of *Kartika* (October-November), considered to be the most auspicious period for this ritual.(video clip)

Below
Asi ghat

Rana P. B. Singh explaining the significance of Lokarka Kunda near Asi ghat (video clip).

ASI MYTHOLOGY BOX

The interface between the city and the river consists of flights of steps known as ghats. The ghats stretch along the river for three miles in the shape of a crescent moon and create a continuous horizon. Banaras has 84 such places, which are defined by landscapes, temples, trees form of worship. Over time, each ghat has acquired its own place, specific myths, and together the ghats provide people with a powerful setting for self-transformation. Once the transformation has occurred, a pilgrim needs to remember the experience.

The Asi mythology box is an aid to remember the pilgrimage experience. Buttons on the box depict symbols of the ghat, mythology, rituals, and allows people to play back images relating to rituals, places, place-specific symbols and interpretations of Asi ghat. Eventually, these boxes when miniaturized could become an electronic amulet that let people connect to the sacred centres of mythology.

Opposite page
Clicking on the mythology box allows people to remember places and rituals on Asi ghat. e.g., the stepped wells of a Sun shrine.

Multi-level Documents
Physical objects could be designed to convey state and meaning. By a transformation of the physical state physical objects become a multi-level display. The world of GUI computing evolved overlapping, cascading windows. By extending this idea into the physical world, a physical display can become a carrier of meaning and information.

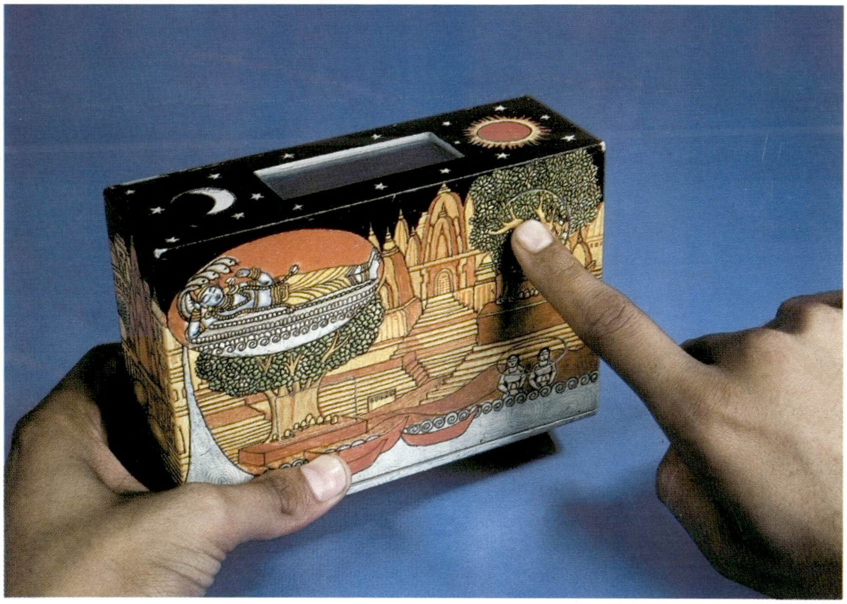

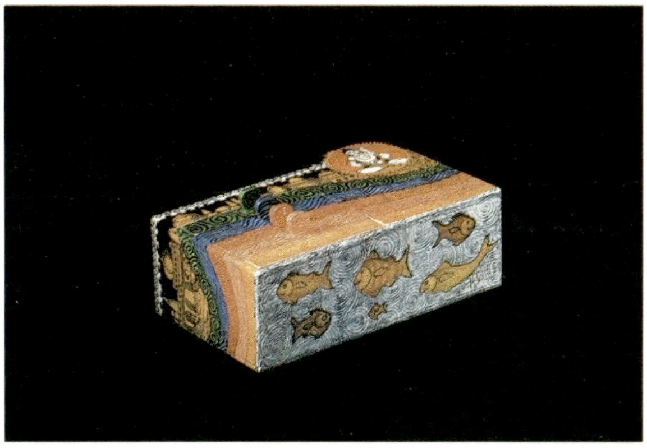

The Tulsi ghat is named after the poet-saint Tulsidas, who lived in the sixteenth century (d 1623). Tulsidas lived at different places in Varanasi in different periods of his life - at Panchaganga ghat, Hanuman Phataka, and the Gopala Temple. It is said that he had a vision of god Hanuman at the site where the temple of Sankata Mochana stands, and near the banks of Asi, in a house which is located in Tulsi ghat.

The ghat has earned its significance from the leagendary visit of Tulsidas to this ghat. The ghat has survived through the memory of Tulsidas and the events, such as the open air Ramalila initiated by the Sankata Mochana Temple. Today it also houses the Sankata Mochana Foundation, an NGO devoted to the cleaning of the Ganga. Further down from Tulsi ghat is the famous Kedar ghat.

Tulsi ghat

Future shrines with embedded displays and interfaces within traditional architecture suggest a vision of digital temples.

WINDOW INTO TULSI GHAT

Tulsi ghat by the banks of the Ganga derives its name from the poet-saint Tulsidas, who composed the *Ramacharitamanasa* based on the epic Ramayana by the banks of the Ganga.

Banaras is famous for its traditional travelling theatre, the Ramalila, based on the legend of the epic-Ramayana of Valmiki. The Ramalila of Banaras captures the sacred geography of the epic in its outdoor locations - hilltops, street junctures, trees, wells, paths - all reflect actual sites of the ancient legend. Tulsi ghat is the venue where the rituals for the Ramalila commence during the autumn festival, which commemorates the return of Lord Rama from his exile. The *Ramacharitamanasa* of Tulsidas is chanted in its entirety as the play travels through different locations in Banaras.

Kedar at Kashi is the centre point of the southern part of Kashi called the Kedar Khand. The temple at the top of the ghat is marked by red and white stripes and a beautiful bathing tank, Gauri Kunda, a water reservoir that adds to its geometric beauty. The pilgrimage site of Kedaresvara lies in the northern belt (*Uttarkhanda*) of the Himalaya at an altitude of 12,000 feet on the banks of the river Mandakini, one of the twelve Lingas of Light (*jyotirlinga*). It is believed that Shiva resides there in his brilliance to bless his two devotees, Nara and Narayana who propitiated him there. The five Pandava brothers are believed to have come there for purification after the Mahabharata war. On seeing them Shiva turned into a bull and disappeared into the earth. Five parts of Shiva's body became visible through the earth and became pilgrim spots as "five Kedars". On account of its importance Kedar is replicated in Kashi and in other parts of India. This auspicious pilgrimage site which lies in the northern Himalaya is replicated in the Kedar Khanda at Varanasi. It is stated in the Kashi Khanda of the *Skanda Purana*, "By seeing Kedara in Kashi one obtains seven times as much merit as obtained by visiting Kedar often climbing the Himalaya." The temple at the top of Kedar ghat by the Ganga houses one of the most primal Shiva linga's in Kashi. The linga is a large rough mound, flat in surface, with a white line demarcating the centre. Legend holds that one day king Madhatri offered *khichri* (a rice and lentil preparation) to Shiva who came in the guise as a guest to test the king's devotion. The *khichri*, transformed into a stone linga of Shiva. Blessed by Shiva's presence in his linga, it became an empowered symbol.

Kedar ghat

As one walks along, one is confronted with Kashi's oldest cremation ground named after the legendary King Harishchandra.

Harishchandra ghat

It all began when sage Vishvamitra asked his devotee, King Harishchandra, for the sacrificial fee (*dakshina*) that the king owed his teacher. King Harishchandra asked the sage to name what he desired. In reply, Vishvamitra asked for the "earth, with its oceans, and with its mountains, villages, and town, and their entire kingdom... whatever else thou possess excepting thy wife, son and body." The king gifted his entire kingdom to his teacher. Accompanied by his wife and son, King Harishchandra left his domain for the holy city of Varanasi.

This and next page
Mural painting (Kerala) depicting the legend of King Harishchandra.

At the gates of Varanasi, King Harishchandra saw sage Vishvamitra who insisted that his sacrificial fee still had not been paid in full. The only way that the king could have fulfilled the sage's requirement was by selling himself. While Harishchandra was pondering over his next step, his wife Shaviya interrupted his thoughts by saying, "There is nothing higher than truthfulness. Being such a man, give me in exchange for wealth and pay the sage."

Driven by sorrow, the king watched an elderly brahmin buy the queen and drag her by the hair as a slave girl. Harishchandra's son Rohit was also bought at a price by this Brahmin.

This wealth was still not enough to pay Vishvamitra's sacrificial fees. The king then offered himself for sale. A foul smelling *dom,* a caretaker for the cremation in Kashi, disfigured, adorned with garlands taken from the corpses, and surrounded by a pack of dogs offered to buy the king. The king was enraged as the man belonged to the lowest caste and refused to give himself up to the man. But sage Vishvamitra insisted that only this man's wealth would suffice his needs.

For a long time, King Harishchandra

worked as a servant at the cremation ground under the *dom* and his job was to gather garments from dead bodies. Each day, he went to the burning ghat in Vanarasi where he was surrounded by vultures, jackals, mountains of bones and the cries of the relatives of the dead.

Then one day, the king saw his wife carrying their dead son to the cremation ground. The queen, worn out with sorrow, did not recognize the king. He looked filthy with matted hair and was totally withered in stature. Overcome with sorrow, King Harishchandra and the queen contemplated throwing themselves into the blazing pyre of their son.

While the couple stood thinking, the gods appeared before them. Lord Dharma, Indra, the rest of the gods, and sage Vishvamitra told the king that they were gratified by his patience, self-command, and sense of virtue. They showered nectar from the heavens, which instantly rekindled life into the dead body. He rose from the pyre in perfect health. The gods told Harishchandra that he had attained life in the third heaven with his family in recognition for his sense of duty.

But the king refused to leave the cremation ground in Varanasi without compensating his former master, the low-caste Chandala. Then Lord Dharma realised that he himself had assumed the form of the Chandala to test the king. Completely gratified by the king, the gods asked him and his family to live with them in the heavens, and free themselves from the bonds of existence.

Mural painting (Kerala) depicting the legend of King Harishchandra. *Contemporary.*

The next significant ghat one comes to is the Dashashvamedha ghat, one of the most popular ghats along the river-front that attracts crowds of people each morning. The ghat is the centre-point where pilgrims gather to perform their respective rituals with the aid of pilgrim-priests (*pandas* or *tirtha purohitas*) who sit there under bamboo umbrellas to administer the rituals. Legend has it that it is here that Lord Brahma performed his ten-horse sacrifice which confers lavish boons.

The southern side of the Dashashvamedha ghat was known by the ancient name of Rudrasavrovara, "Lake of Rudra". The northern sector of the ghat is known as Prayaga ghat, named after the famed Prayaga tirtha, (now referred to as Allahabad) at the confluence of the three rivers: Ganga, Yamuna and Saraswati. This is Prayaga-in-Kashi and its spiritual powers are exactly the same as the one situated in Allahabad.

The ghat has three important lingas which pilgrims who undertake the Panchatirthi pilgrimage are advised to visit. They are first, Shulatankeshvara, which marks the northeastern boundary of Kedara Khanda, second, Brahmeshvara, established by Lord Brahma, and third, Dashashvamedheshvara in the compound of the flat-roofed Shitala Temple. This is the ghat which is linked directly to the Vishvanath Temple and its complex of smaller shrines. Close to the Vishvanath Temple is Jnana Vapi "the well of enlightenment", 10 feet in diameter, and is the place where pilgrims come to sip water and make a vow of intention (*samkalpa*) before they commence a pilgrimage in Varanasi. It also marks the spot where the pilgrims return at the end of their journey.

Opposite page
Dashashvamedha ghat

THE DASHASHVAMEDHA MYTHOLOGY BROWSER

The Dashashvamedha is one of the most popular bathing ghats along the river-front. Millions of pilgrims and worshippers come to take a holy dip and purify themselves from their accumulated impurities, physical and psychical.

The mythology browser allows people to browse through the multiple layers, symbols, myths, and rituals of the Dashashvamedha ghat through the physical act of information retrieval. The browser engages the user at a human scale as the user moves a digital lens upon a mural. The lens detects hotspots of information on the mural and displays interpretations and meanings on the screen. Such types of large browsers engage the whole body in the act of information retrieval.

Dashashvamedha ghat depicted in mural painting in Kerala style. *Contemporary.*

Just as people point on hotspots on the glass screen of a computer display, the mythology browser allows people to point on a physical display. In doing so, the browser reverses physical and virtual displays. The physical mural underlying the lens is the display and the digital lens which overlays the graphic, the cursor.

Shrine of Annapurna

ANNAPURNA BHAVANI

Like Vishveshvara, the king and the presiding deity of Kashi, goddess Annapurna is the queen, who governs and rules the sacred city. She is also referred to as Bhavani or the female shakti of Bhava or Shiva. She is a gracious deity, who as her name suggests, is abundant with food which she bestows freely to one and all. She is depicted holding a cooking pot and a ladle. In popular posters, Shiva is shown receiving alms from Annapurna and depends on her for his sustenance.

Shiva and Annapurna together fulfill the most basic needs of sacred life: Annapurna, food for sustenance, and Shiva grants liberation. According to a popular legend sage Vyasa once cursed the city that it would go without knowledge, wealth or liberation for three generations. Vyasa begged for alms at the residence of Shiva and Paravati, who were residing there as householders. Paravati invited the great sage and his attendants and feasted them with a delicious meal. Vyasa forgot his curse and proclaimed: "who would not live in Kashi where one can get both delicious food and liberation". It is widely accepted that because of the generosity of Annapurna no one ever starves in Kashi. However, the significance of Annapurna is much deeper than the giver of food. By virtue of the fact that she nourishes the devotee, she also supports and grants him liberation.

Shrine of Annapurna.
Legend holds that the present shrine of Annapurna was established by a poor brahmin, Dhanajaya, who was instructed by the goddess Annapurna to observe her fast (*vrata*). However, no one could inform him as to how the fast was to be observed. He travelled to Kamakhya, where he had another dream in which the goddess instructed him to establish her image in the form of Annapurna to the south of the Vishvanatha Temple. She further proclaimed that she would grant all wishes to those who observe her *vrata*. It is held that the goddess came from Kamakhya to feed and bless all of Kashi.

The present shrine of Annapurna is situated close to the Vishvanatha Temple on the opposite side of the lane.

VISHVANATHA TEMPLE

Shiva is Vishveshvara, the lord of the universe, the presiding lord of the city where he is recognized through his symbol, the *Jyotirlinga*, the Linga of Light which is synonymous with the city of Varanasi. The heart of Banaras is the Vishvanatha Temple where the *Jyotirlinga* is installed. The establishment of the present shrine of Vishvanatha has a long and chequered history. As early as AD 1194, the site was marked for destruction by Muhammad Ghauri's captain, Qutb-ud-din Aibak. By AD 1236, the site instead came to occupy a mosque built by Razzaiyyat-ud-din during her short reign. The golden dome of the temple was constructed on a massive scale in AD 1585 by Narayana Bhatta with the patronage of Todar Mal, one of Akbar's courtiers. However, the fate of the temple was shortlived. It was razed to the ground by the Mughal emperor Aurangzeb. This becomes a site for the mosque near Jnana Vapi. The Shiva linga that was enshrined here was considered to be desecrated and so consigned to the well. In 1777, the Queen of Indore, Ahalya Bai sponsored the construction of the present temple, as it stands today, with the *Jyotirlinga* in the sanctum.

The next major ghat which represents Kashi's most significant sacred geography site is the Manikarnika ghat, the well-known cremation ground in Kashi. Its oldest association is with Lord Vishnu who carved out the world's first *tirtha,* a lake with his discus and filled it with the perspiration of his austerities. Today, the large lake is a sacred well, called Chakra-Pushakarani Kunda. The Manikarnika Kunda is located in the north of the cremation ground. The Manikarnika is known as Mahashmashana, because the funeral pyres eternally burn here and never cease to exist. This is the holy spot where people surrender their earthly bodies and receive the spiritual body of Shiva. It is here that Shiva, likened to the boatman, utters the liberating Taraka mantra and carries the souls to heaven, just as a boatman ferries the boat across the shore. It is here that the final "crossing" over from the realm of material existence to the realm of transcendence takes place.

Manikarnika ghat

THE MANIKARNIKA MYTHOLOGY BROWSER

Every stone of Kashi is impregnated with layers of meaning, but our eyes only see the physical level, irrespective of the layers of mythology embedded in the places of the ghats. Hence the Manikarnika browser is designed as an "eye", a physical display that allows people to unravel the mythology of the mural below it.

Mural painting (Kerala) depicting the Manikarnika ghat

The mythology browser allows people to unravel layers of the myth of the Manikamika ghat. Displays are not static. Displays can be moved, and with the impending advent of wireless information readers, displays with embedded position sensing can allow people to discover meanings of underlying physical objects.

Positioning the lens on hot spots on the mural allow people to retrieve interpratations of scholars and artists which are displayed on the lens.

Amongst all the ghats in Varanasi, the most sacred is the Panchganga ghat. This ghat is situated at the confluence of five holy streams - the Ganga, the Yamuna, the Saraswati, the Dhutapapa, and the Kirana. It is believed that a dip in this holy intermingling of waters sets a person free from the unceasing cycle of rebirth. A reason why everyone in Varanasi reveres Panchaganga ghat is because this ghat is associated with the lives of many famous intellectuals and philosophers. Ramananda (16th century AD), guru of Kabir used to live and visit this place. Shankaracharya also had his famous conversation with Lord Vishvanatha disguised as a low-caste man on this ghat. Poet Jagannatha (17th century AD) wrote his ode to the river Ganga on this ghat called the *Ganga Lahari.* In terms of the sacred geography of Varanasi, this ghat is important as it is the starting point of Vishnu Kashi which extends up to the Adi Keshava ghat.

Panchaganga ghat

Adi Keshava ghat

The last at the northern end of the river bank, the Adi Keshava ghat is situated on the bank above the confluence of the river, Varuna and the Ganga.

The Adi Keshava, named after the"Primal Vishnu" is said to be the spot where Lord Vishnu first set his holy feet when he arrived in Kashi. According to ancient belief the city of Kashi by the river is identified with the five bodily parts of Vishnu. The Asi ghat is the head; Dashashvamedha is the chest; Manikarnika, the navel; Panchaganga, the thighs, and Adi Keshava, the feet of Vishnu. An important site in Adi Keshava is the Sangameshvara Linga, which is located in a temple in the ghat.

ADI KESHAVA MYTHOLOGY BOX

Throughout the world, prayer beds and amulets allowed people to remember their sacred centres. The Adi Keshava Mythology Box painted with symbols of Adi Keshava, Vishnu's home in the ghats, allows people to access the rituals and myths of Adi Kesava ghat. In a real time mode, such a box could allow pilgrims to to be connected to the rhythms and rituals taking place on the ghats.

Physical objects could be designed to convey state and meaning. By transformation of the physical state, physical objects can function as a multi-level display.

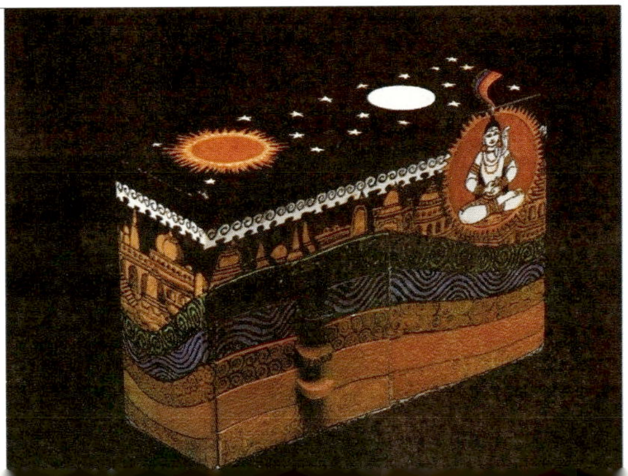

On account of their sacred geoscape, the ghats provide and mark specific pilgrimage routes for the pilgrims who come to Kashi. Some of the major ghats not only shrine smaller *tirthas,* pilgrimage sites, but provide the benefit of going on a long pilgrimage. One of the most important pilgrimages is the route where the pilgrims cover the entire length of the river bank. One of the most popular one is the Panchatirtha yatra, the pilgrimage to the five major ghats: the Asi ghat, from where the journey commences, the Dashashvamedha ghat, Adi Keshava and Varuna river confluence at the northern tip of the river front, the Panchaganga ghat and finally to the Manikarnika ghat. At each of these way stations, the pilgrims have a holy bath, and a darshana of the most important gods who are installed on the ghats. After the yatra, the pilgrims return to have a darshana of Kashi, Vishvanatha. From a distance, to the contemplative devotee, the crescent-shaped ghats are identified with the luminous crescent adorning Shiva's matted locks, and the river Ganga flowing like a stream of consciousness in the imagination of the devotee is like the nectar of immortality that flows from Shiva's crescent moon. The ghats then hold together the healing and purifying waters of Ganga who is personified as a mother goddess.

Ganga

Banaras is unique because here the divinity is accessible not only through temples, altars, saintly people, and places, but through the river Ganga who is symbolized as a mother goddess, a divinity in natural form. The river Ganga is the life-line of Kashi's landscape. The holy river and Shiva have an enduring relationship. Ganga is considered to be the co-wife of Paravati, the other daughter of the Himalaya, Himavat. Ganga is the consort-goddess of Shiva who issues from his matted locks.

In this epithet, Shiva is known as Gangadhara, the bearer of Ganga. One significant myth of the birth of god Kartikeya represents him as the son of Ganga (*ganga-putra*), or one born from the Ganga (*ganga-ja*). Shiva cast his seed in the fire which was later received and nourished in the womb of river Ganga. A. K. Coomaraswamy (*Yaksas* Part 2: 55) regarded that originally Ganga was a "river-spirit" derived from the *yaksha-dyad.* With the passage of time the "river-spirit" was anthropomorphised and given a distinct iconographical identity. She rides a crocodile and holds two jars of water in her hands. But her icons vary from place to place. In Bengal she is depicted as a woman in white, seated on a crocodile (*makara*). In her right hand she holds a lotus and in her left a lute. In South India, she is shown as a mermaid, swimming in water with folded hands, bearing a Shaiva mark on her forehead. In Banaras, her icons are carved on the ghats where she is depicted seated on her vehicle, while her natural liquid form of river embraces the icon.

Considered to be the most sacred of all rivers, the Ganga is regarded as a purifier of sins, giver of health and fortune, and bestower of salvation, her flowing waters create a natural beauty, which induces contemplation, peace and serenity.

Statue of goddess Ganga by the ghats.

Goddess Ganga floating on a fish. *Rajasthan, 20th century.*

Hindu devotees seek her blessings at all times. The symbolic meta identities that Ganga embodies are founded on its unique geological features. Rich in minerals, her waters remain pure inspite of the pollution that surrounds it today. All through history, the beauty, magnificence and splendour of Ganga have been eulogised by India's greatest saints, poets, philosophers and writers.

This perennial river, old as the mountains, emerging as a thin icy trickle, gushes through the deep Shivalik gorges shaped by mountain crests and elevated plains to Haridwar, also called the "Gate of the Ganga". The river then rolls eastwards, where she breaks out into the plains, the Prayaga, where she joins the rivers, Yamuna and Sarasvati, to Kashi, where she runs through the north as if turning its course to its source. In its easterly course, the Ganga collecting the waters of the Yamuna, the Gomati, the Gagra, the Sarada, the Gandaki, the Sone, the Kosi, the river rolls southeast into the northern plains and merges into the Bay of Bengal.

Opposite page
Ganga descending from the mountains.

The Ganga embodies an entire theology in her silent currents. Kalidasa described her as, or the liquid essence of Lord Shiva *(shambhorambhormayimurti)*, saint Ramakrishna said Ganga waters reflect the supreme Brahman, the absolute principle in the form of water. Legend holds that Ganga existed in the heavens as the star Paladeus, as a divine stream - as *ambhas* or the causal waters of creation in the Milky Way. Beyond the heavens, supported by cosmic space, she is known as Akasha Ganga. She was brought down to the earth by sage Bhagiratha. Her mighty currents swept through the worlds, until Shiva held her in his matted locks.

Ganga issuing from Shiva's locks.
Folk style, Rajasthan c. 20th century.

Priyadarshini Govind performing the Bhagiratha myth of the descent of the Ganga in Bharatnatyam style.(video clip)

The Descent of Ganga

The story of the heavenly descent of the Ganga is found both in the Vaishnava as well as the Shaiva versions. The central myth is related in the *Ramayana* (*Bala Kanda* 38-44), the *Mahabharata* (3.104-108), the *Skanda Purana* (*Kashi. Khanda.* 30) and the *Narada Purana.* There are several versions of this myth. In one popular version from a Vaishnava source, the origin and descent of the heavenly river, Akasha-Ganga to earth takes place from the "foot of Vishnu" (*Vishnu Pada*). The holy river had its origin in the heavens when Vishnu, in his Vamana, dwarf-cum-giant incarnation measured the three worlds with his three steps. While taking the third step his toe pierced the heavenly vault and caused the water to flow through the crevices produced in the shell of the cosmic egg. Through the opening in the shell of the universe, the Ganga flowed into Indra's heaven, and settled around the immovable pole-star, Dhruva. In this form Ganga is known as *vishnupadi.* She meandered through the sky to the moon as the Milky Way. The Milky Way is often referred to as Akasha-Ganga and suggests the idea of a heavenly river.

The next episode of the myth taken from Shaiva sources describes the descent of the Ganga on earth. The story consists of long episodes. The heavenly Ganga descended to the earth for salvic purpose, namely to animate and purify the 60,000 sons of Sagara, who were reduced to ashes by the glance of sage Kapila. The Ganga was brought down to the earth by Bhagiratha who performed fierce austerities on the Himalayan slopes and won the favour of the goddess. She agreed to descend but warned Bhagiratha that the earth would split under the torrential currents of her fall. Ganga asked him to placate Shiva. Shiva agreed to catch its gushing waters in his matted locks before releasing the waters. The mighty river wound her way through Shiva's ascetic locks and found her course on the mountains and plains of India.

Bhagiratha then led the Ganga to the nether world where her purifying "funeral" waters liberated the 60,000 sons of Sagara. In the nether world, Ganga is called Bhogavati, from which the waters were raised for Bhishma by Arjuna who pierced the nether regions with his arrow. Bhagiratha then conducts her to the sea. With its waters the sea was replenished. After completing her course of the three worlds, the mother of the holy rivers returned to the heavens. Oral myths also reflect the vitality and richness of legends that are centred around the Ganga. A popular myth from the Himalayan region gives a vivid account of the origin of ten streams of Ganga in the Himalaya. Once, Paravati closed the eyes of Lord Shiva with her tender lotus-like fin-

Descent of Ganga
The penance of sage Bhagiratha and the release of Ganga.
Kangra style.
19th century.

gers. The world was plunged into darkness when Shiva's eyes that pour light into the sun, moon and fire were closed. Nothing was visible and a great catastrophe fell on the world. Goddess Paravati became frightened and perspiration began to flow from her tender fingers. The perspiration of Paravati, transformed into ten streams with innumerable sub-streams and rivulets. Shiva then opened his eyes and gave light to the world. This caused a great disturbance in the environment. The Gods prayed to Lord Shiva and asked him to avoid another catastrophe. Lord Shiva brought all the rivers and their branches into his matted locks.

In another myth from Vaishnava sources, the *Brahmavaivarata Purana.* (*Prakriti Khanda* 9) describes how Radha and Krishna become Ganga in Golaka, their celestial paradise.

Once on a full moon night in autumn, Shri Krishna was worshipping Radha in a *rasamandala.* Many celestial gods were honouring the gods. Sarasvati played the lute, vina. Lord Shiva began to sing songs in praise of both of them. Hearing his songs, all the demi-gods fell into a swoon. When the gods woke up, they saw that the entire *rasamandala* had been flooded with water and Krishna and Radha too melted and disappeared. The gods called out to them and then they heard a voice from the sky saying that "both me (Krishna) and my Shakti of bliss have transformed into water of Ganga". Then Krishna said, "the water that has emanated from me and Radha is a bestower of pure *bhakti,* which is why the entire universe worships Ganga."

Rituals by the Ganga

On the ghats one encounters the essential Banaras of popular imagination. Pilgrims bathing in waist-deep water offering oblations with cupped hands, ritual priests (*pandas*) sitting under shaded bamboo umbrellas, performing rituals, priests chanting holy verses to the river goddess, people taking boat trips hailing Shiva, pilgrims sprinkling holy water on the body of deceased relatives and sadhus performing yoga. These enactments, though happening today, take us further back into primal time, when nature and humans were in harmony.

Because of the sacred significance of Ganga, and its undisputed efficacy, a number of rituals are performed by the banks of the Ganga in Banaras. These rituals are described in the *Narada Purana*. They range from simple holy dips to elaborate cultural festivals on the Ganga. Some major rituals are: *Darshana*, the beatific or auspicious sight of the goddess Ganga. It is said that a mere sight of the Ganga purifies. In India, the auspicious sight of the deity holds special significance. Even casting a faithful gaze on goddess Ganga in her natural form as a sacred river brings good luck to the observer. *Sparsha*, touching the sacred waters; *Pana*, drinking the sacred waters; *Snana*, bathing and taking a holy dip in the sacred waters; *Smarana*, contemplation on the glory and significance of Ganga; *Vrata*, observing special vows by the side of Ganga, like fasting, etc., *Tapas*, performing special penances, such as recitation of mantra while standing in water, performing fire rituals (*homa*) by the banks of

the Ganga. Recitation of the Ganga *Mahatmya:* singing, reciting and listening to the greatness or glory of the Ganga on the banks. The sacred word plays a very important role in religious life. From the great poet Valmiki, (c. 4th century AD), the author of the great epic, the Ramayana, to the philosopher Shankaracharya, and many poets of distinction, in the modern period, have written hymns on the glory of Ganga. The eulogies dedicated to Ganga are looked upon as sonic theologies. Chanting these hymns is considered to be a holy performance.

Ganga *arti* at Dashashvamedha ghat.(video clip)

Ritual worship (*ganga-puja*) of the river is identical to the form of worship that takes place in private shrines. Five ritual ingredients, such as flowers, incense, lamp, grains and food-offerings are offered directly to the river. Lamps are floated and worship is performed to the chant of mantras. From the customary dawn rites (*sandhya*), to dusk, the evening *sandhya* — all forms of daily devotions are performed by the Ganga. The dawn rites at day break commences with certain purificatory rites, when the shimmering light of the sun touches the water. It consists of offering water to the gurus, ancestors and to the deities. The same ritual is repeated at mid-day and at dusk. All the daily purificatory rituals are performed on the banks of the Ganga, or standing in the waters. Apart from these daily purificatory rites all the important life-cycle rituals, such as the baby's first bath, tonsures, the bath before marriage and the death ritual are performed on the banks of the Ganga. Nothing is holier for the Hindu than performance of the funeral rites in Kashi by the side of the Ganga. The ancestors of Bhagiratha only after being purified by the sa-

cred waters, were able to reach to the other world. Likewise, all mortals need to be freed, lest they live in limbo as negative spirits causing harm to the living. The water of the Ganga is called "*amrita*" or the nectar of immortality and thus has the potency to bring new life to the dead. Thus the pilgrimage to Kashi normally includes rites for the dead. This includes the performance of the elaborate funeral rites (*sraddha*) after the death or a more abbreviated form of rites performed at any time. The rite consists of offering rice balls (*pinda*) to the ancestors while the hymn of their names is chanted. This brings great joy to the ancestors.

Each year on the tenth day of the month of Jyestha (May-June), the great celebration dedicated to mother Ganga takes place. This is a yearly festival. This festival commemorates the day when Ganga descended on the earth and is regarded to be her birthday. It is referred to as *Dashmi-tithi* (tenth day / dusshera) because of the "ten" astrological conjunctions that take place on that day when the Ganga descended on earth. They are:

(1) *Jyeshta* the month of May-June; (2) the bright fortnight; (3) the constellation *hasta*; (4) Wednesday; (5) *Dashmi-tithi,* the tenth day of the bright fortnight; (6) *gara-karana,* the significator of the constellation (*gara*); (7) *ananda yoga,* the specific yoking point which bestows bliss; (8) *vyatipata,* nodal point of celestial equator; (9) *the moon in the* zodiac sign, Virgo (*Kanya*), and (10) the sun in the zodiac sign, Tauras (*Vrisha*).

Snana, holy bathing

Darshana, beholding the Ganga

Sparsha, touching the holy water

Japa, recitation of Mantra

Marraige ritual

Death rituals

This day marks that primal moment when the Ganga rolled down from the heaven to the earth as a great gift of the gods. The symbolic meaning of number ten is explained. On this day bathing in the Ganga destroys ten types of sins (*dasha-vidha-papa-hara*) rising from the body (*kayika*), speech (*vachika*), and mind (*manasika*). According to yet another interpretation, Dusshera destroys "ten life-times of sins" committed by humans or all sins accumulated through several lives. This is one of the three auspicious days in Kashi when people vow to bathe before dawn. This is meant to be "pleasurable austerity" as they delight in the "cooling" goddess Ganga in the beginning of the hottest of seasons. Some people celebrate this day by crossing the river on boats trailing along a garland of flowers to adorn the river goddess.

Dana or offering charity is a practice which is considered to be very crucial to the Kali age. The Ganga itself was bestowed to the earth as a great gift (*dana*) by Shiva to Bhagiratha, and through Bhagiratha, the whole of mankind. The Ganga is honoured by the worshippers who in turn recycle the splendours of the earth, even their own body, as a gift to the holy waters. In this ritual act, the sacred river is a witness to the ritual event and bestows her blessings to the bestower.

Tapas, performing penance

Yoga

E-POTS

Mythology and Interface

Throughout the world, pots have been seen as auspicious symbols of the goddess. The pots in their subtle form suggest the fertile womb, and mirror the forms of our body. Holding the pot evokes a feeling of tenderness and compassion. The E-pot allows users to access the creation myths describing the descent of Ganga from the heavens to the earth, the artistic interpretation of the moods of the Ganga, as well as the discourse on whether nature bodies are a physical or psychical phenomenon.

The interface is not purely a functional object. Like icons in traditional arts, they serve as both a representation and extension of the object of interaction. Moreover, in many ritual traditions, artists through carefully generated representations of iconometry trap nature's energies. Many objects are related to subtle bodies, relating through correspondence ordinary tools to highest idealizations. Ganga first flowed in the heavens in her subtle form before coming down to earth.

Goddess Ganga holding a water pot and a lotus.(detail).
Folk style, Banaras. 20th century.

Ganga E-Pots

Integrating the body posture in the interface, the e-pot allows people to experience the Goddess Ganga and her qualities of compassion by holding the pot.

Ganga E-Pots

Mind vs Matter Pots

In the pot, an image of Ganga is split into two halves. One suggesting Ganga as divinity and the other as a physical substance, H_2O. The user interacts with these pots to explore how the physical aspect of water becomes divine as a fertility bestowing goddess.

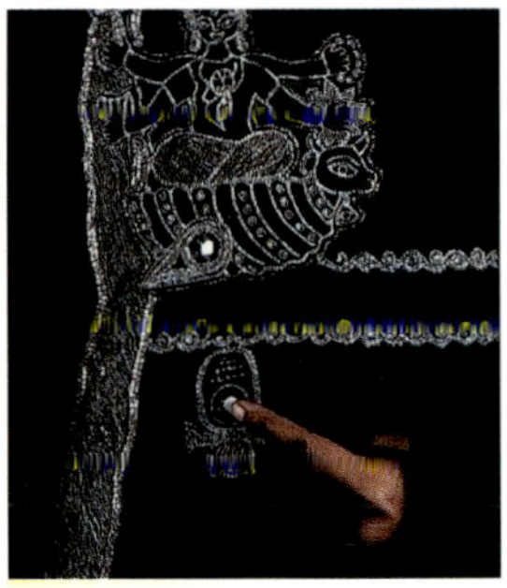

E-JACKET

Wearable computing

Pilgrimages show us a rich space of traditional media. Portable shrines, adornments, amulets, and necklaces scaffold the pilgrim to enter and remember transformative experiences. Wearable computing could restore these dimensions.

The world of ritual tradition speaks of *Nyasa*, a system of communication and ritual purification through which the yogi establishes correspondence between the world without and the world within. By having hotspots on jackets, wearable computing allows people to click on themselves, and remember the links between the outer and inner worlds.

Stills from the E-Jacket

The yogi meditates by the river reflecting on the correspondence between outer and inner elements. Clicking on the embroidered buttons on the e-jacket allows the yogi to internalize the elements, the lights, the forests, mountains, man-made cosmos and ultimately the "Ganga within". Wearable computing allows people to carry our symbols but, more importantly, it allows people to click on themselves.

E-Jacket

Wearable computing allows pilgrims to carry their sacred city while on the move. The portable image, whether icons or prayer beads or amulets, address an important need found in all strata of society to connect to sacred centres.

E-MASK

The E-Mask is an attempt to combine "bits" and "beads". Beads of a Chau mask have been substituted by LED lights. Together, grids of LED lights create a display screen, which display the mantras of the goddess Ganga. By incorporating simple displays and interfaces in traditional crafts, a new genre of e-crafts is explored.

Intellectual Traditions

Throughout the centuries literature and cities have shared a special symbiotic relationship. Modern metropolitan cities carry the complexity and tension of modern life. The creativity they inspire bears a special genre of literature of discontent and tension, conflict and existential angst. In comparison Kashi, the ancient city of enlightenment, revels in a generative environment of traditional learning. As early as the 7th century B C, the sacred city became the focal point of increased intellectual and spiritual activity; and since then has flourished as one of the greatest centres of traditional learning and of established theological and philosophical discourse.

Banaras is a "living scripture" of Hindu thought. Throughout its long history Banaras has attracted an astounding variety of visitors. Apart from having an unbroken tradition of *Shastric* learning, Banaras probably had the largest number of ashrams of ancient India which were the traditional universities of wisdom and enlightenment. Over a period of time, Banaras emerged as one of the greatest centres of classical learning in India and attracted a whole generation of students from all over India to study the Vedas. It is not surprising that Banaras is often referred to as *Brahmavardhana,* a place where knowledge of Brahman increases. The word Kashi (from the Sanskrit *Kasha,* to shine) too reflects the same meaning, the place where the essence and nature of Brahman is illumined. The ghats of Banaras provided for an open-air university where India's greatest philosophers, thinkers and pandits held debates and pondered over the meaning of existence. Kashi was not only the seat of orthodox Hinduism, but the city got appropriated by all the sectarian sects of India, the Jainas, the Buddhists, the Shaivas of all denominations, the Aghora Tantrics, Gorakhanatha Panthis, the Natha and Siddha saints, the popular *bhakti* cults and a variety of popular unorthodox sects whose norms run counter to orthodoxy.

The city also attracted leading exponents of different schools, religious seekers and ascetics who found this to be an ideal place for their spiritual pursuit. In the post-Vedic ferment of the rise of new religious and philosophical orders, Banaras became the fountain-head of learning. Acharya Baldeva Upadhyaya in his monumental work, *Kashi ki Panditya Parampara,* traces the life histories of a generation of traditional scholars and intellectual luminaries who made significant contribution to traditional learning through their writings. The works of

Sangvedavidyalaya, a traditional school for Vedic learning in Varanasi.

the traditional pandits in Banaras cover almost all schools of philosophy and theological discourse in India. Naturally, by design or desire, the sage-scholars and pandits in Kashi, acquired a distinctive quality. The city provided for an intellectually stimulating atmosphere, a lifestyle dictated by the virtues of simple living and high thinking, and a spiritual environment, which provided, above all materialistic concerns, an ambience to pursue a pious life that guaranteed *moksha.* The pandits of Kashi were well known all over India for their mastery in *shastrartha,* or debates in traditional learning. Their intellectual talent was all the more enhanced by their nobility of conduct, humbleness, and talent in meticulous articulation of Vedic chanting. These features made Kashi a renowned centre of traditional learning. Scholars from all over India came to Kashi to draw from its dynamic and prosperous intellectual heritage.

Several great works glorifying the pilgrimage site of Kashi were written there. Of the many such *Mahatmyas,* the most well known is the *Kashi Khanda,* containing 11,624 verses. Scholars date this work to the c. AD 1300. It is one of the seven *khandas* "sections" of the voluminous *Skanda Purana.* The *Kashi Khanda,* it is believed, was compiled to gather together and document the important sites of the cultural geoscape of Kashi - the innumerable micro- level *tirthas,* along the river, the *lingas* and *kundas* (water sources) that are found all over the city. The text also gives copious information on the origin of well-known sites, such as the Manikarnika kunda, and the Dashashvamedha ghat. The work also eulogises the inherent part of the sites through legends and describes at length the rituals that are to be performed by the pilgrims around the year. In similar vein, two later texts compiled in the 17th century are worthy of mention. The *Kashi Rahasya* in 26 chapters gives an esoteric interpretation of Kashi, and the *Kashi Kedar Mahatmya* is a eulogy on one of the three sacred zones of Kashi, the Kedara Khanda, located in the southern sectors of the city. These works reveal the importance the city acquired in the post mediaeval period. The sacred authority of Kashi's tradition of Sanskrit learning also inspired non-Hindu kings to acknowledge and contribute to its streams of learning. A case in point is the example of Dara Shikoh. During his reign he sponsored the translations of the *Upanishads* into Persian by employing pandits of Kashi.

Not only did Kashi provide the subject and content of scholarly discourse in the religious digests, but the city inspired great scholarly activity among the community of pandits in Kashi. An influential figure of great historical significance was Lakshmidhara, the chief minister to king Govindachandra in the mid-twelfth century. Single-handedly, Laksmidhara is known to have inspired a new era of Hindu religious literature by compiling a voluminous digest (*nibandha*), *Kritya Kalpataru,* in 14 volumes. His commentaries according to Eck (1983:32) exemplify "a theory of Hindu Pilgrimage". Another scholar of significance was Narayana Bhatt, an active scholar-statesman in the sixteenth century who is credited with the authorship of *Tristhalisetu,* a digest on three famous pilgrim centres in North India - Kashi, Prayaga and Gaya. Narayana Bhatt is historically recorded to be the main force behind the reconstruction of the Vishvanatha Temple in 1508.

Along with this some ghats, such as the Panchaganga ghat and Tulsi ghat yielded to the rise of poetic literature. The 15th and the 16th centuries saw the resurgence of the *bhakti* movement in North India and once again Banaras was centre stage in this movement. Banaras produced some of the most outstanding *nirguni bhakti* poets who wrote about reality beyond name, class and creed. Saint Ramananda emerged at the advent of this new

KABIR

creed preaching his message of devotion to the illiterate, the downtrodden and the outcastes and an outright distaste for the orthodox Brahmanical culture of India. Ramananda lived on the Panchaganga ghat and gathered around him great poets, such as Kabir, Dadu and Raidasa. Kabir, who is regarded as one of the greatest of all poets, was from a low-caste Banaras weaver's class. His writings vehemently opposed any forms of organized religion, sacred books, idolatory and the Hindu Kashi. His followers created a great centre after his name in the city. In the 16th century, Banaras gave birth to another great poet-saint of *bhakti* tradition Tulsidas, who wrote his famous version of the *Ramayana* named *Ramacharitamanas* in Hindi renowned to be the most popular classic in the Hindi-speaking belt. Pandit Jagannatha, inspired by the beauty of the ghats, wrote his famous work *Gangalahari* on this ghat in the 17th century.

In comparison with the urban Indian cities, Banaras has retained its ancient flavour, both in its architecture as well as style of life. On account of its ageless character and spiritual identity, the city has attracted along with the pilgrims an astonishing number of foreign visitors, travellers, merchants, civil servants and missionaries who have recorded their personal reflections about the city in their respective works. The first to be traced historically is Parashavanatha, the twenty-third Jina, *tirthankaras*. "Ford-makers" who was born in Kashi in the 8th century B.C. From then to the current period, the Jainas of both denominations, the Digambaras and Shvetambaras have continued their traditions. The most important seeker to visit Kashi was Siddhartha Gautama who came to be called the Buddha, the "Awakened One". After he attained enlightenment, he set out for Varanasi to impart his teachings that have come to be called the Four Noble Truths and one Eightfold Noble Path. He came to a park which is called Rishi-patana for the "sages", and also "Mrigadaya", "gift to the Deer", named after the Jataka tale in which the king of Varanasi gifted a park to the deer. In modern day, the place is called Sarnath. Here the Buddha attracted his first lay followers and set in motion "the wheel of dharma". Buddha is said to have spent his first rainy season retreat at this spot. A monastic retreat (*vihara*) was established for nearly 1,500 years. Sarnath has been one of the most important monastic centres of Buddhisim, visited by pilgrims from all over the world. In the 4th century BC the Buddhist emperor Ashoka built a great stupa there. Between the 4th and the 6th centuries, Sarnath was to emerge as a great centre of Buddhist art. Haun Tsang is said to have chronicled that there were 30 monasteries and 3000 monks who lived there. Over the years Varanasi became increasingly famous as a seat of Buddhism until the 12th century when the Kutb-ud-din Aibak armies attacked and demolished Sarnath.

Well-known travellers, such as an English visitor Ralph Fitch (AD 1584), Jean Baptiste Tavernier (AD 1668) a French traveller, a jeweler by profession described the Bindu Madhava Temple as the "Pagoda". Similarly, Bishop Reginald Hever and Emma Roberts from Britain also came there. Two of the most well-remembered visitors were Mark Twain, who in his around the world travelogue, "Following the Equator" describes Banaras in vivid terms, sometimes with great humour. The most well-known visitors to Banaras were the two British architects, Thomas and William Daniell who were forced to make a stop over at Banaras. They sketched some memorable scenes of the Banaras riverfront. Their artworks preserve the 18th century landscape, lined with the green cover, that was transformed as the urban centre shifted to the southern part of the city.

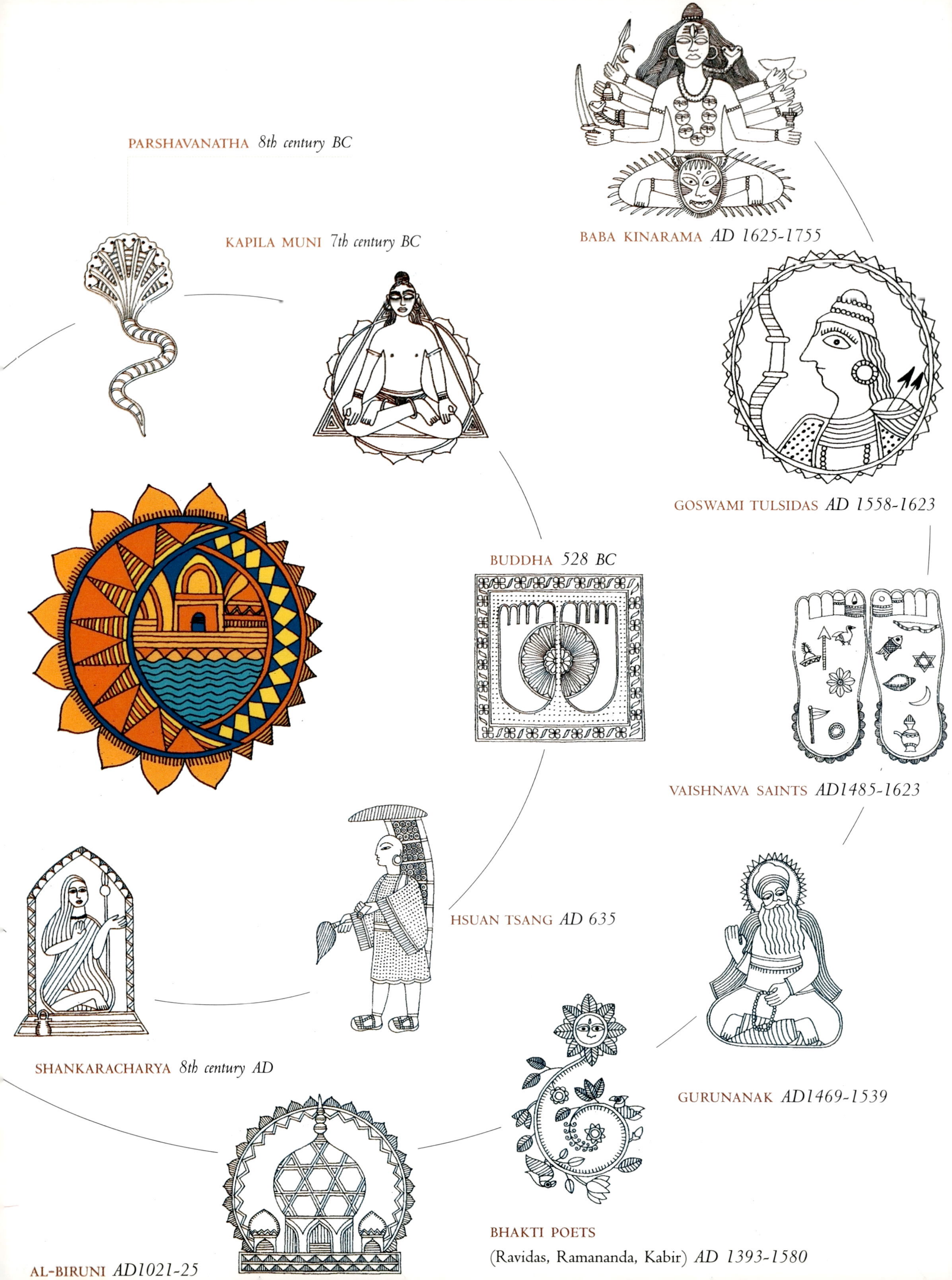
PARSHAVANATHA 8th century BC
KAPILA MUNI 7th century BC
BABA KINARAMA AD 1625-1755
GOSWAMI TULSIDAS AD 1558-1623
BUDDHA 528 BC
VAISHNAVA SAINTS AD1485-1623
HSUAN TSANG AD 635
SHANKARACHARYA 8th century AD
GURUNANAK AD1469-1539
BHAKTI POETS
(Ravidas, Ramananda, Kabir) AD 1393-1580
AL-BIRUNI AD1021-25

DARA SHIKOH *AD 1656-57*

THOMAS AND WILLIAM DANIELL *AD 1788-89*

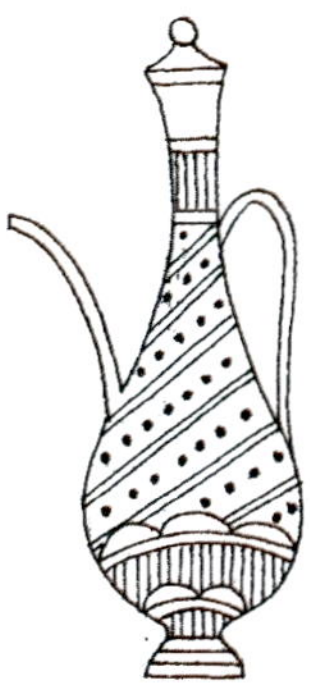

MIRZA GHALIB *AD 1797-1869*

RAMAKRISHNA PARAMHANS *AD 1868*

MAHATMA GANDHI *AD 1930-36*

THEOSOPHISTS (Annie Besant, Krishnamurthy)
Mid 20th Century

MARK TWAIN *AD 1895*

SWAMI DAYANANDA SARASWATI *AD 1869*

Jina Parshvanatha

Banaras is the birth place of the 23rd tirthankara who was born in 800 BC. Tirthankaras are enlightened while living and are the founders of the four-fold order of monks. Parshvanatha is said to have attained enlightenment in Kashi.

Sadhavi Bhavyananda on Parshvanatha(video clip).

Kapil Muni

Sage Kapil (7th century BC), the founder of the Samkhya philosophy lived and wrote his great work, *The Samkhya Sutra* in Banaras. This work forms the philosophical basis of the classical yoga discipline taught by sage Patanjali.

Vagaish Shastri on Kapil Muni (video clip).

Buddha

Siddhartha Gautama Buddha was born in the 6th century BC as a wealthy prince of the Shakya clan. He left his palace in search of truth and enlightenment. After Buddha attained enlightenment, he delivered his first sermon to five disciples at Sarnath which is 10 km from Banaras. He preached the Four Noble Truths that outlined the middle path for attaining "Nirvana".

Sandong Rinpoche on Buddha (video clip).

Huan Tsang

Huan Tsang (AD 635), the celebrated Chinese pilgrim, made a sixteen-year pilgrimage to India in order to learn about Buddhist teachings. During his journey from AD 629-645, he travelled an astonishing 10,000 miles in search of Buddhist scriptures. He visited Sarnath where he got a replica made of the famous teachings of Buddha.

Lokesh Chandra on Haun Tsang (video clip).

Al-Biruni

Al-Biruni, the great astrologer-astronomer (AD 1021) travelled to India and visited Banaras in search of knowledge.

- Lokesh Chandra

Shankaracharya

The great Shankaracharya (8th century AD) came down to the city of Kashi and wrote a commentary on *Vedantasutra*. This is known as *Sharirakabhashya*. In Kashi he encountered an outcaste, a *chandala*. He asked the outcaste to stay away from the street. It is maintained that the outcaste posed a certain question to him: whether he wanted to be away from his body or soul—the soul, which is omnipresent and all-pervasive. Then Shankaracharaya realized that it was in fact Lord Vishvanatha himself asking him this question in the guise of *chandala*. Shankaracharya went on to write the *Manishapanchaka*, in which he maintains that if a person is aware of the true nature of the *atman*, then such a person, even if he was an outcaste, was his guru.This interesting work is a testimony that Kashi taught the great Shankaracharya the real meaning of the *Vedantasutras* which led to his writing an inspired commentary.

K D Tripathi on Shankaracharya (video clip).

Guru Nanak

Nanak was the first *guru* of the Sikhs. About AD 1500 he experienced what he claimed was revelation of god. This led him to declare that "there is no Hindu, there is no Muslim". This realization marked the beginning of his mission. Nanak travelled widely and in 1563 he visited Banaras. He began to sing praises of God, with Mardanaji, who was accompanying him, and soon enough a large crowd collected to listen to him.

Kashi is a holy city and many religious scholars have emerged from here. At that time several scholars in Kashi were quite proud of their learning. Pandit Chatur Das was one such

A sevak on Guru Nanak (video clip).

scholar. When he learnt that Guru Nanak had come to Kashi, he went to meet him along with his disciples, and held a long drawn philosophical debate with him. The great sage got tired of him and asked him why he was following him like a dog. As the sage spoke, the pandit turned into a dog. He begged forgiveness, till the great sage told him that he would be released the day Guru Nanak comes to Kashi and blesses him.

Ravidas

It is well known that even today, Banaras pays homage to Ravidas, one of the eminent *nirguna* bhakti-poets who is regarded as a catalyst for all those who aspire after the "uplifter of the fallen", the "master of the meek". Born in Banaras, a cobbler by birth, he was one of the most precious voices who excelled in the controversies with the upper caste brahmins of Banaras. The brahmins in Banaras were shocked to find that a low-caste cobbler had stolen their thunder. It is said: "Ravidas, the *chamar* praised God and every moment sang the praises of the one God. Though a fallen *jati,* he became exalted and all four castes came and fell at his feet". *(Callewart et al, 1992: 11)*

A huge, newly constructed hall stands on the northen end of the ghats near Adikeshava ghat to mark the memory of this humble, yet great soul.

Chaitanya Mahaprabhu

Sri Chaitanya (c.1485-1534) was the founder of the Vaishnava sect popular in Bengal. He preached his path of love through singing, and chanting the name of god (*kirtana*) as aids to ecstatic communio between god and the devotee. This form of worship came to be known as *sankirtan.* Chaitanya was violently opposed to the doctrine of Shankara and Vedantins. When Lord Chaitanya came to Banaras with his travelling *sankirtan,* many disciples of Sripada Prakasananda Sarasvati (a Vedantic *mayavadi* scholar) attracted by the transcendental chanting, joined him. Chaitanya held many theological debates with *mayavadi* sanyasis, especially Prakasananda at Banaras. Chaitanya's commentary on the philosophy of chanting the supreme mantra of Krishna convinced the sanyasins of Banaras about the efficacy of the bhakti tradition. In no time, the whole city of Varanasi began to praise him. Today, there is a small temple of six-armed form of Lord Chaitanya in Jatan-para recalling his visit to Varanasi.

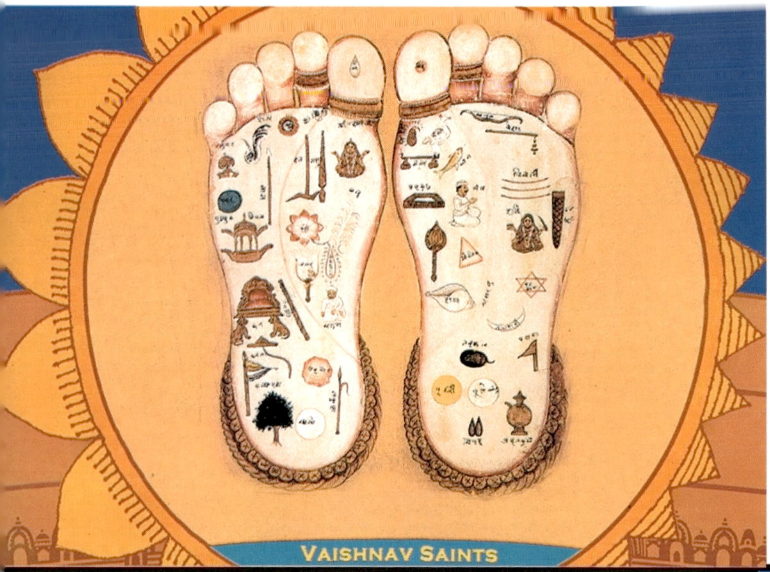

Shuk Deo Singh on Kabir (video clip).

Kabir

Kabir ranks among one of the greatest poets. A weaver by profession, his poetry is a fine blend of Hinduism and Islam into a single faith. In Kashi, Kabir creates one sacred space within another and adds to the importance of this holy city with his immeasurable contribution. Kabir believed that there is no need for sciptures, temples or mosques, for where Kabir stands, God himself will find you.

In Banaras, Kabir was greatly tested and went through rigorous trials before he became known as one of the most profound philosophers and saints of our times. Like the river Ganga changes her course in Banaras and begins to flow in the opposite direction, so too, Kabir's philosophy went against the current to emerge as an alternative faith stream, where religion had no name and God existed in the hearts of one and all.

Goswami Tulsidas

Tulsidas (AD 1558-1623) spent his last years in Banaras or the sacred land of Varanasi. He started writing the last part of the *Ramacharitmanas.* It was with the grace of *Hanuman* that he had a full vision of Rama, a vision of reality that he had not had before. The greater portion of the *Kavitavali* and *Hanuman Bahu* were also written here.... It has been rightly remarked by many western scholars that the *Ramacharitamanas* has a larger audience than the Bible. Being in Banaras he became involved in staging Ramlilas. Almost the entire text of the *Ramacharitamanas* is incorporated in the Ramlila. In this great performing theatre the audience are not the spectators, but the active participants of the play.

Vidya Niwas Mishra on Tulsidas (video clip).

Aghoracharya Baba Kinaram

Banaras is not only the seat of orthodox tradition but was a home of several unorthodox traditions of Hinduism. The Aghora, a Shaivite sect was one of them. The name of the sect is of extreme antiquity and is traceable to one of the five faces or manifestations of Lord Shiva in his Aghora form.

One of the illustrious personalities in the history of the Aghoras was Baba Kinaram. This tradition is said to be dormant since the time of Aghori Bhairavacharya (5th-6th century BC). Baba Kinaram (b. 1658) was one of the most well-known saints in Banaras of this lineage.

The Aghoras are generally characterized by their indifference to orthodoxy. They reject the Vedas, scorn caste and flout any form of rigid convention. The word, Aghora literally means "that which is not difficult or terrible". Aghora is simply a natural state of consciousness. It is about bliss in oneself, a coming close to one's own divine soul.

Baba Kinaram established an ashram in Banaras, called "Krim Kund" at Shivala. He initiated many social reforms during the tumultuous times of the Mughul invasion when Hindus were being persecuted. The direct lineage of the twelve Aghoreshvaras that began with Baba Kinaram extends from the 16th century until the present.

Thomas and William Daniell

The Daniel brothers (AD 1788-89), made three epic journeys, one which took them from Calcutta to the Himalaya. On their way out from Calcutta they went to Banaras, sailed down the Ganga and created those famous pictures of the waterfront at Banaras. A number of painters came down to India at that time because they got good commissions and their paintings were worth a lot when they went back to Britain. To people in Britain, India seemed to be an exotic land a world that they had never seen. The Daniels were remarkable draughtsmen; they had extraordinary representational skills, almost photographic yet much richer than what photography can offer.

Mark Tully on Thomas and William Daniell (video clip).

Prince Dara Shikoh

Prince Muhammad Dara Shikoh (AD 1627-1658), the favourite son of Mughal emperor Shah Jahan ruled over the kingdom of Oudh (Awadh). He was a Sufi mystic, unorthodox in terms of his outlook, and a free thinker. He had deep knowledge of Sanskrit and had studied original Hindu scriptures. Dara Shikoh employed the pandits in Banaras to translate Sanskrit scriptures in Persian. His translations included the *Upanishads, Bhagavad-Gita* and *Yoga-Vashistha*. At Banaras, he completed his monumental work *Sirr-ul-asrar* (also known as *Sirr-i-Akbar*, meaning the Great Mystery), a translation of 50 Upanishads, on 1 July 1657 AD. It was titled, "The Upanishads: God's Most Perfect Revelation".

Gopichand Narang on Mirza Ghalib (video clip).

Sri Ramakrishna Paramhansa

Ramakrishna Paramhansa came to Banaras around 1868-69 with one of his devotees who was an aristocrat. From the time when Sri Ramakrishna entered Varanasi by boat, he saw with his spiritual eye that the city of Shiva was actually made of gold. He stayed near Kedar ghat. In Varanasi, Ramakrishna visited temples and ghats along the Ganga which often threw him into *samadhi*.

One day as he was passing by Manikarnika ghat, (the most important cremation ground in Banaras) in a boat with his nephew, he had a vision of Lord Vishvanath. This vision made him ecstatic.

RAMAKRISHNA PARAMHANS

MIRZA GHALIB

Mirza Ghalib

There is no one who doesn't know who Ghalib (AD 1797-1869) is. They say he is a good poet, but an infamous poet. Ghalib is universally recognized as one of great minds India has produced. His poetry is complex. His poetry is marked by enigmatic qualities, yet Ghalib is a poet of exquisite charm. He was so inspired by Banaras and he wrote a long poem in Persian, called *Chirag-i-Dair* or Temple Lamps.

"May Heaven keep
The grandeur of Benares, arbour of bliss,
Meadow of joy,
For oft-returning souls
Their journeys end.
In this weary Temple-land of the world,
Safe from the whirlwind of Time,
Benares is forever spring...

....The Kaaba of Hind, this conch-blowes' dell!
Its icons and idols
Are made of Light...

...My Lady Kashi
Plucks up the Ganga-mirror
To see her gracious beauty
Glimmer and shine."

(translated by Qurratulain Hyder, cited in the *Taj Magazine*, First Quarter, 2002, pp. 32-33).

Dayananda Saraswati

Dayananda Saraswati, the founder of Arya Samaj, regarded the Vedas as the eternal, unfallible and most perfect revelation of the sages. His purpose was to shed superstitions and disbeliefs and to revive the Vedic religion based on Yaska's *Nirukta,* the text on etymology. He was fiercely opposed to polytheism and idolatry. He travelled widely and spent a great part of his life in rescuing the sacred text and expounding the Vedic faith. Swami Dayananda visited Kashi to teach his new Vedic philosophy. In Kashi he stayed at Anandabag owned by one Raja Madhava Singh. This spot is known for the historic debates he held with a galaxy of pandits of Kashi on the question whether idol worship is sanctioned in the Vedas or whether the word *pratima* "icon" or *murtipuja* "worship of idols" occurs in the Vedas? History records that these debates proved his mettle as a foremost reformer and leader of the Arya Samaj through which he carried the message of the Vedas and of universal brotherhood to humankind.

Vachaspati Upadhyaya on Dayananda Saraswati (video clip).

Pandit Madan Mohan Malaviya

Pandit Madan Mohan Malaviya (b.1861) was a great patriot, visionary educator, social reformer and a great statesman.

His most monumental achievement was the establishment of the Banaras Hindu University (BHU) or the Kashi Hindu Vishwavidyalaya. This university which was founded in February 1916, rose to great heights and is recognized as one of the great centres for learning across the world. Malaviya chose Banaras as the site for his dreams because of its unbroken tradition of learning, wisdom and spirituality. The university offered the teaching of science and technology along with religion. He envisioned the integration of the best of Indian education with the best traditions of modern universities from the west. The Colleges of Agriculture, Engineering, Mining, Metallurgy and Geology, the Ayurvedic College and an Allopathic Hospital were started in BHU. This made it pre-eminent among the contemporary Indian universities. Annie Beasant, Mahatma Gandhi, Rabindranath Tagore, Maharajadhiraj of Darbhanga and Maharaja of Banaras were among the other visionaries who made this effort materialize in the quest to arouse the spirit of nationalism in India.

Annie Beasant

When Annie Beasant came to India (AD 1820), she had a great vision of the spiritual, moral and political regeneration of India. Banaras became a cornerstone for Annie Beasant's great project. She moved to Banaras and started the Indian section of the Theosophical Society in 1896. What Annie Beasant wanted to do was to create a new model of education. She wanted to create a new human being by combining ancient wisdom with modern European knowledge. To this end she started many institutions in Banaras, the most important of which was the Central Hindu College. Soon this college had more than a thousand pupils. It was actually the germ from which the Banaras Hindu University was formed later with the help of Pandit Madan Mohan Malaviya and others.

Markand Paranjape on Annie Beasant (video clip).

Rajiv Vora on Mahatma Gandhi (video clip).

Mahatma Gandhi

Gandhi's mission could be explained in several ways but basically he came as a saviour of India, to free India from the British rule.

Banaras has a very special place in Mahatma Gandhi's life, in India's life and in the development of his personality and his thought. In his childhood, he saw a play on Raja Harishchandra, who was as idealistic king. Harishchandra's greatest test of truth happened in Banaras according to legend. Harishchandra's story deeply influenced Gandhi's philosophy. Mahatma Gandhi came to Banaras in the first week of February 1916. He made a historical speech in which, for the first time, he made a statement on the state of India. This happened on the day the foundation stone of Banaras Hindu University was laid.

E-PADUKA

The guru's feet has been associated with feelings of respect and sense of preciousness. Students often wash the guru's feet and adorn the feet with lotus petals. Can modern media capture such feelings of preciousness? The e-paduka, with its really ornate carved forms, allows people to access the teachings of the gurus of Banaras.

THE NEED FOR ORNAMENT

Abstract forms of technology, e.g., key board pads disappear and reappear in culturally meaningful forms. With the progressive rendering of our world abstract by information technology, "embodiment" and "visualization" of information becomes important. Individual signature and the ability of a community to personalise forms of information access becomes important in the face of globalization.

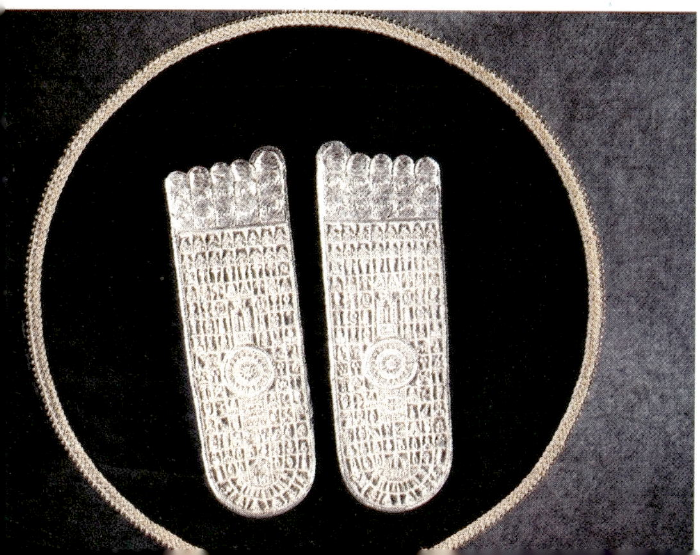

MAHAYAMA GANDHI 1930–1936

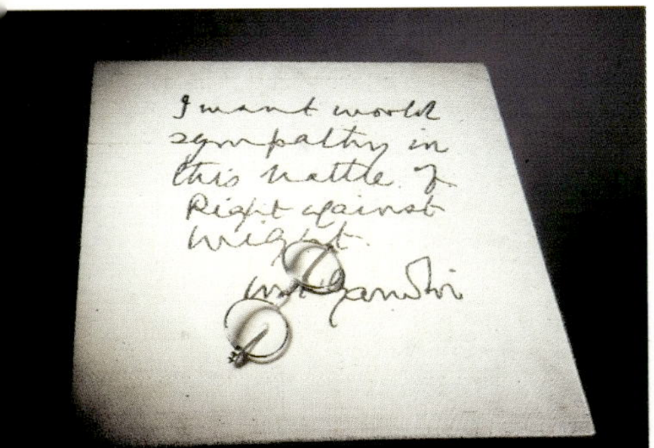
I want world
sympathy in
this battle of
Right against
Might.
M K Gandhi

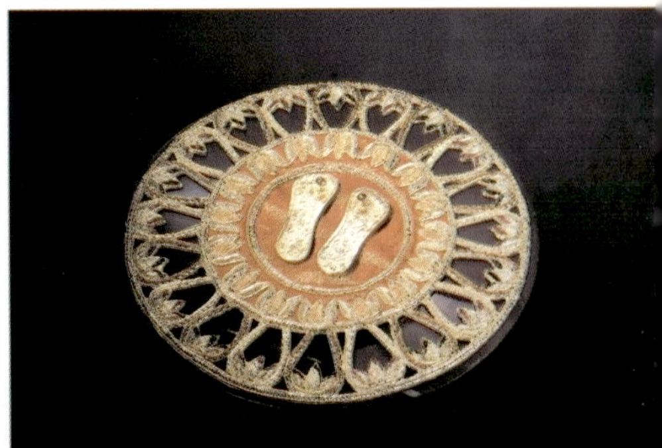

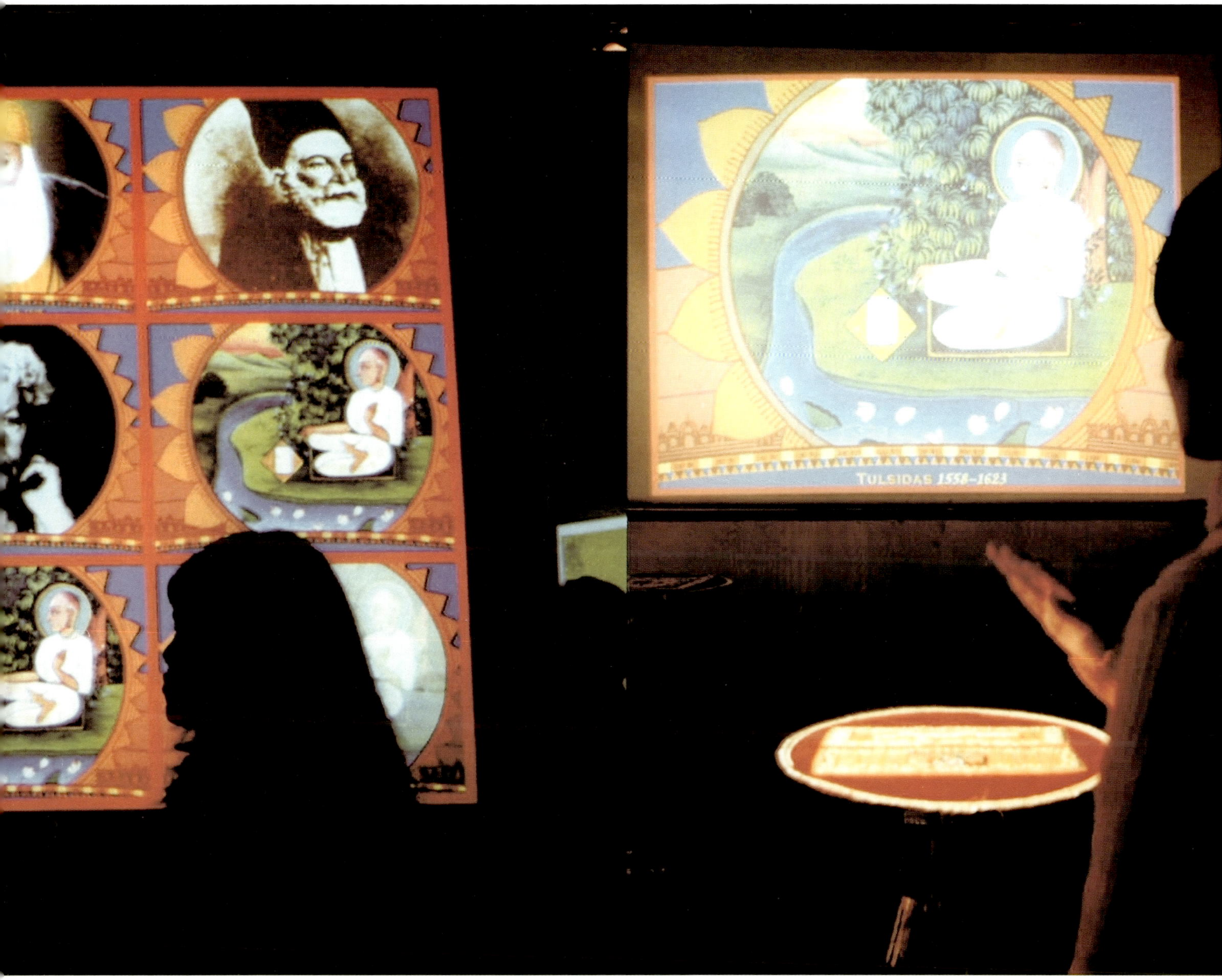

E-PADUKAS

Using a traditional symbol of worship such as the padukas of the guru, the e-padukas evoke the feeling of respect for the gurus in Banaras.

death

" People think that Banaras is about death. There is death everywhere. The burning bodies on the ghats, the half burnt corpses floating down the river...But Banaras is not about death, it's about eternity..."

Raja Rao

In the Hindu view, living and dying are both considered to be joyous. There is a very thin line separating the two conditions of the soul. Death is not feared or looked upon with danger, impurity or terror. It is seen as a condition that recycles the elements and takes the soul on its destined path. The horror linked to the phenomenon of death is dispelled as death is taken as a state of enlightened illumination. Indeed, death loses its sting in Banaras and is a state of restored beneficence brought about by the presence of Shiva. Iluminating the significance of death, Diana. L. Eck (1983: 325) states, "Death, which elsewhere is under a terrifying jurisdiction of Yama, is free from terror here, for Yama is not allowed within the city limits of Kashi. Death, which elsewhere is polluting, is here holy and auspicious. Death, the most natural, unavoidable, and certain of human realities, is here the sure gate to *moksha.*"

The reward of spiritual liberation *moksha* that Kashi offers cuts through barriers of caste, class and geographical boundaries. The rewards are not merely for Hindus but for Muslims, Christians, foreigners and even non-believers.

The Manikarnika cremation ground is the famous "burning ghat" where the burning pyres never cease. The ghat is active round the clock, day after day, non-stop. It is held that Shiva gave a special boon to Kashi, as the *Skanda Purana* (Book 4 Section I, Chapter 30, 95-97) explains: "Whatever their number, all beings that stay in Kashi, in water or on ground, fish, jackals, etc. have the body of Rudra, due to my blessings...All who die in Kashi become immortal." People from all over India come to Kashi just to die a good death. They come for *Kashivasa* or "living in Kashi" until their mortal frame drops. It is believed that this is the last stop on earth on their pilgrimage to enlightenment. There are others who are terminally ill or at the brink of death, who come to Kashi for accruing the benefit that Kashi brings. They make it just on time to attain *Kashilabh,* "The benefit of Kashi". Such people are usually brought to charitable homes, such as Kashi Labh Mukti Bhawan, where dying is made easy and peaceful. In such homes, no medicine is given, as the patients come here not to recover but to die in the presence of Shiva. They are given sacred *tulsi* (basil) leaves and pure Ganga water, the finest of the natural drugs for healing. It is believed that Shiva stands like a teacher and guide at death's door. When the final hour arrives, Shiva himself appears in an invisible form and whispers the liberating Taraka mantra in the ear. The Taraka mantra is said to be "the ferry-boat mantra". It is a sacred formula which enables the individual to cross over the ocean of material existence. It is believed that in the city of Kashi, Shiva himself assumes the form of a universal guru who liberates all those who seek a refuge in Kashi. The miracle mantra is

"All who die in Kashi become immortal whether they are rabbits, mosquitoes, cranes, parrots, sparrows, wolves, jackals, horses, serpents, monkeys or men."

Skanda Purana Part 4, Section 1, Chap. 30, Verse 7

communicated to the dying directly, almost instantly without any human or godly intervention. Shiva is the "death-bed" teacher and guide here.

Shiva whispering the Taraka mantra.
Kerala mural painting (detail).

In the great *Mahatmyas* of Kashi, it is held that in the celebrated Manikarnika cremation ground, the dead assume the form of Shiva and mysteriously acquire his posture and emblems. In the likeness of Shiva, the dead embody the three eyes of Shiva, adorn their hair with a crescent moon and hold a trident. Shiva stands in the cremation ground and transforms the base matter into his very divine essence. This transformation is brought about by the immortal sacred fire in which the corpse is sacrificed as an offering to Shiva. This union with the godhead is read as a bestowal of grace of Shiva who is ever ready to bless and liberate humankind from the ocean of material existence.

At death, the individual habits a liminal space somewhere between complete cessestion of life and death. This state of the soul in transition is known as *preta,* a soul that has left the mortal frame and has yet not attained a new birth. Death rituals are performed to free the soul from this transitional state so that he may transform into a *pitri,* ancestor, and finally attain his own destination according to his *karma.* The death rituals consists of:
(1) Purification and bathing of the corpse in the Ganga.
(2) The corpse is then sprinkled with fragrant oil and adorned with flowers.
(3) The fire is lit by the chief mourner with a flaming wad of Kusha grass from the Dom's eternal fire. The fire is circumambulated anti-clockwise as everything is flowing counter to the positive-life governing rhythms of life.

(4) The fire is lit and the burning corpse is looked upon as a supreme offering to god Agni.
(5) The rite of cracking the skull *(kapala bheda)* takes place which symbolically releases the soul from the poisoned body.
(6) The ashes are collected by the mourner and immersed in the Ganga as a final act.
(7) The chief mourner takes a large earthen pot filled with Ganga water and throws it backward over his left shoulder. For the next eleven or thirteen days, daily offering of rice balls *(pinda)* are made with a feast to the brahmins, who symbolically partake of the food offered to the dead. On the last day the departed soul is said to have reached its final destination and joins the ancestors.

Death ritual being performed at the Harishchandra ghat.

In Kashi, the deity presiding over death and human destiny is Kala Bhairava, embodying the personification of Shiva that surpasses the jaws of death and time. According to a popular legend, when Brahma tricked Shiva after he appeared from the Linga of Light, Shiva created from his anger and fury his fierce form as Bhairava, and decapitated Brahma's head. Bhairava roamed the earth as a destitute and observed the *Kapala vrata* "vow of skull" using the skull as a begging bowl. The head clung to him until he reached Kashi. All this while, dancing frantically pursued by his heinous sin, until in a leap he overcame the dread and terror of Time *(kala)*, and Shiva became Mahakala, one who transcends Time. It is said that "Shiva as Vishvanatha is the king, Annapurna is the queen and Kala Bhairava is the *Kotwal* " The Governor" who guards the territory of Kashi and vigilates over the deeds of all those who

Icon of Kala Bhairava.
Kala Bhairava Temple, Banaras.

Shiva in the form of Kala Bhairava.
Wall painting, Kala Bhairava Temple, Banaras.

live in Kashi. His place is the Kapalamochana Tirtha, where he devours the sins of people. The relatively modern temple of Kala Bhairava was reconstructed in the 13th century. Kala Bhairva is to be worshipped by all those who visit Kashi. His main function is to dispense justice to all those who die there and to administer with the "punishment of Bhairva" *(Bhairava yatana)*, where the dying people experience the accumulated results of their *karma* in a flash.

The sacred city of Kashi is described as the Great Cremation Ground and is synonymous with the idea of auspicious death. Kashi is described as a city shining from Shiva's incandescent light, yielding a lustre *(jyotir)* that engulfs the city. At the abstract level of cognition, the luminous aura dispels the darkness of ignorance. On a more earthy plane, cosmic light manifests as a form of *agni* or fire, which is an element of Shiva. Agni's function is to illuminate as well as to consume and reduce everything to ashes. In Kashi's two famous burning grounds—The Harishchandra ghat and the Manikarnika ghat—Shiva is embodied as *agni*, the immortal fire emanating from the pyres of the dead on the burning ground. Along the ghats glittering with flames rising from the pyres of the dead flow the replenishing waters of the holy Ganga. Water and fire are the two most predominant elements of Hindu cosmology symbolizing the cyclic act of creation and destruction. Fire consumes, water replenishes. Fire reduces all beings and elements into ashes; water fecundates the remnants and is the occasion of new life. These two elements though appearing to be in opposition with one another form a seamless complementarity. No where in the world does the perpetual presence of death embodied by the burning ghats, and the simultaneous presence of life-giving substance, the holy waters intersect so vividly as in Kashi. The sacred fires burn eternally and it is the flames of these fires that are most sacred for lighting the funeral pyre. In a more sublime vision, the fires that leap up from the cremation pyres in Kashi are likened to the sacrificial ritual fires into which the human bodies are offered as an oblation to Shiva for their final deliverance. While fire consumes and "devours" the body, the waters of the Ganga recycle the mortal frame into its root elements and imbue it with new life. Kashi reverberates between the dynamic flux of life and death.

"The sucession of life and death goes on. People come and go. Someone died and left today, someone yesterday, and someone else is preparing to leave tommorow. Everyone has to go, on this one path.
I don't have any fear, death does not scare me at all.I desire death.

-Gayatri Devi (vedio clip).

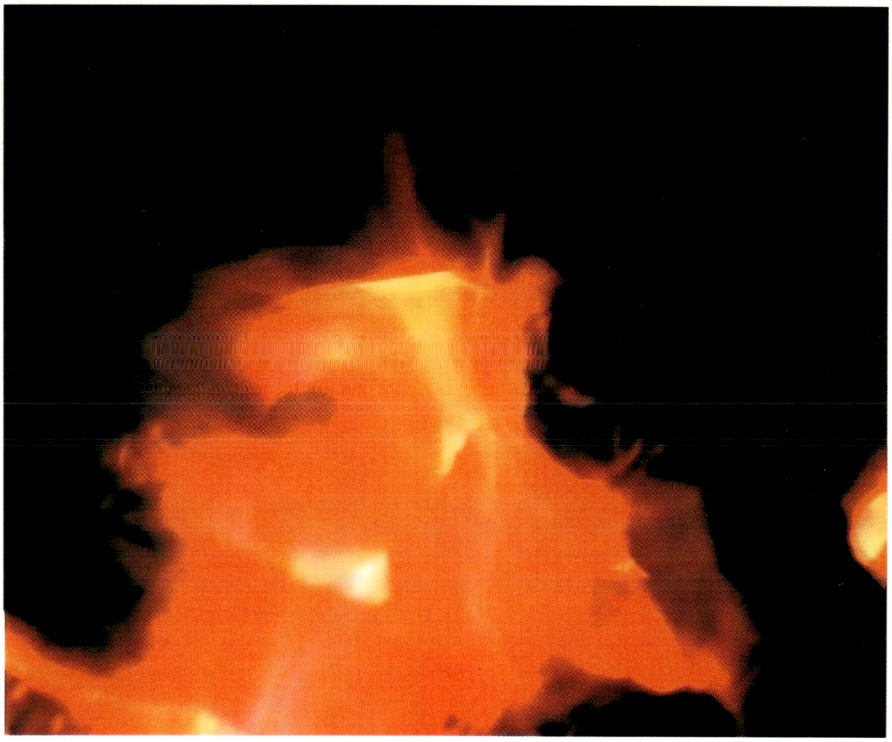

Madhu Khanna on the symbolism of water and fire as related to Kashi. (video clip).

The all-consuming cremation fire blazing on the Manikarnika ghat symbolizing death and dissolution of the elements into their primal source (video clip from the film "Fire").

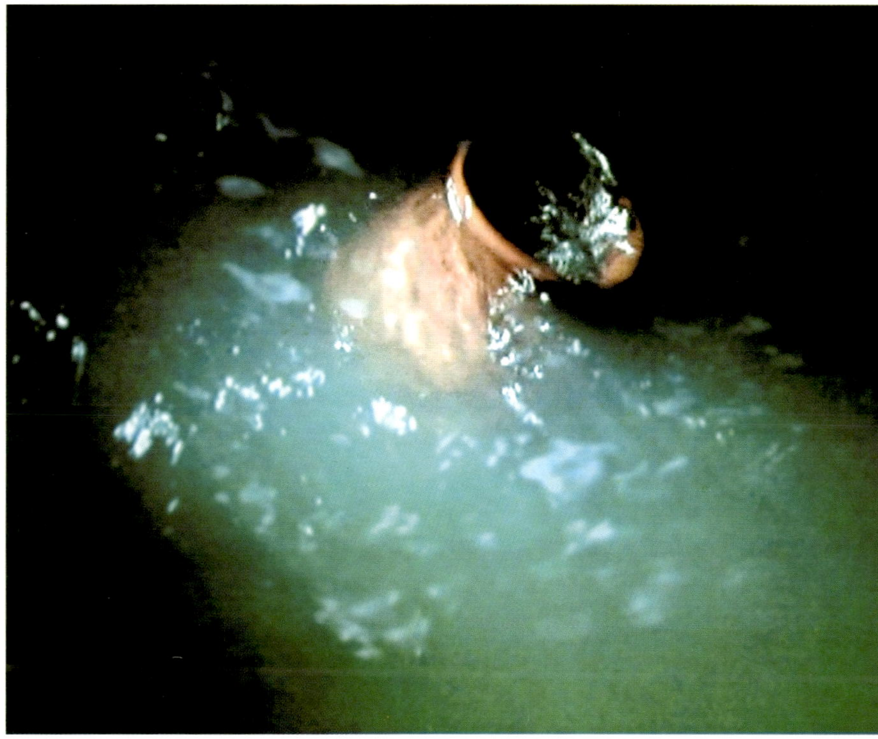

The life-generating waters of the Ganga, symbolizing life and recycling of the elements (video clip from the film "Water").

E-DEATH EGG

The dance of life revolves around the mystery of death. The river-banks of Banaras provide us the spaces for the dying to leave the world of Samsara. For those alive, it allows us to ponder over the question of death. The death egg allows us to understand multiple dimensions of death, from the famous burning ghat, the Manikarnika, to the symbols of fire and water, to discourses on the nature of the body.

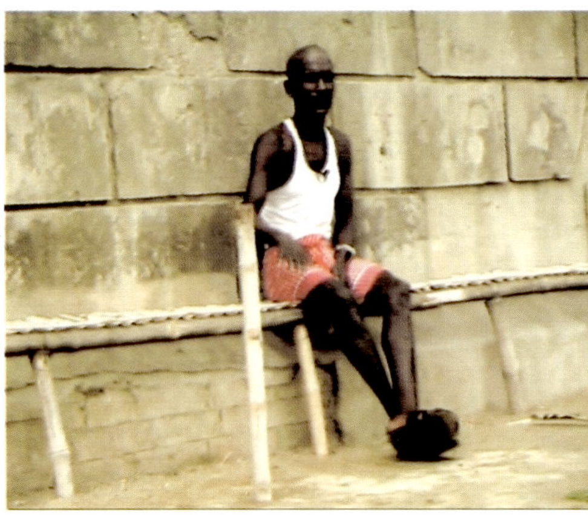

"Seeing the grinding stone turning, turning
Kabir began to weep
Between the two stones, not a single grain is saved!"

Babul Lal, a citizen of Banaras, explains the significance of death in Banaras quoting Kabir (video clip).

Manikarnika ghat

Perspectives on Death

SWAMI VED BHARTI
ON VEDANTA AND DEATH (video clip).

E-Death Egg (opposite page)
Just In Time Healing

With the advent of mobile technology, it is possible to carry life-affirming messages while on the move. Of all the fears in the world, the fear of Death is the one universal fear that grips us all. However, we die only once and must not let the fear of the fear take over death itself. In the Indian mind, all forms of fear are considered to be irrational. While medicines have created solutions for symptoms of anxiety, a crucial problem for people is the timely access to knowledge. Prayer beads and amulets function in a traditional society as remembrances of man's highest ideals. Similarly objects, such as the death-egg can help people to understand the strategies for coping with the fear of death. At a deeper level, the problem of death is related to the problem of the "I" and the body. Buttons on the e-egg allow people to access discourses on the nature of the body and perceptions about an inter-connected man. This discussion critically questions whether the appearance of a separate "I" is a form of perceptual illusion.

I am always puzzled by the mention of the word "death", because when I look around the spiritual life and world, I don't see any such thing as death ever happening. There is no such thing as death.

But people want to understand what the phenomenon is. The fear of death is called in the *Yoga sutra,* "abhinivesha". I've translated that as an obsession with a particular type of thought. This fear is nothing but an obsession. According to sage Vyasa, it is an obsession with "that we may cease to be". On the question of death, there is no such thing. Because, who dies? The body? The body is a system of chemical compounds. All the compounds of the body can be taken together and sold for about 110$. This is the value of the human body. So who dies? The chemical compounds decompose. Now, people have this habit of saying: "Is there a soul inside me?" The question is: who asks that question? The chemical compounds in the body cannot ask that question. The soul cannot say, "Is there a soul inside me?" So who asks the question?

We speak in our tradition of different kinds of death.

The involuntary *karmically* forced death, when we do not know how to infuse fresh "*prana*" into the system of chemical compounds because in the *Upanishads* it is said, we do not live by the ingoing breath (*prana*) or the outgoing breath (*apana*) but by some other force (*na pranena na apaanena martyo jivanti kaschana itarena tu jivanti yasmin etau upasthitau.*). Not only do we not live by the chemicals, (*annamaykosha*) the bread alone if one might say, but we do not live by the air alone either, not by the outgoing breath or the ingoing breath, but we live by something else, some other force which is the result of all of these forces. We have an involuntary *karmically* forced death, which most people suffer and fear because the momentum of *karma* comes to an end and like any motion when the momentum stops, the motion stops, it disintegrates; the kinetic energy vanishes. Inertia takes over.

There is another death, many people are not aware of it, that is death by initiation (*diksha mrityu*). This is one of the very high yoga dikshas in our Himalayan tradition, in which the master takes the disciple through the experience of dying. This is the kind of experience that Raman Maharishi had without a guru. At the age of thirteen, he was in his room and thought, "What is this thing called death that everyone fears?" Let me see what happens." So he lay down and died and he saw this being of light looking down at him. He wondered why people were so afraid of it. I have some use for the body yet; I think I'll stay awhile.

There is that. So, this kind of a death may occur from intangible sources, which is very rare as in the case of Raman, a Maharishi. It may be given to one in ten or twenty million people, usually those living in caves, or sometimes they make exceptions for householders. They take you through the experience, where the body is lying there, and you, the being of light are here.

And the third is daily death in meditation. Samadhi (deep meditation) comes in that category. I call this the daily dose of death, daily vaccination. When you are vaccinated with a small amount of a disease then you build up a resistance. So a deep meditator dies everyday for five or ten minutes. That dying may be done in two ways, sitting in a meditation posture or what we call *shavasana,* or the posture of the corpse. Many people who are teaching yoga today talk of *shavasana,* and after a series of physical postures, they tell the students to lie down in the corpse position. That is how they stop, but the internal work begins there, and goes all the way to *yoganidra* on the one hand, and on the other hand to the art of dying; the art of dying skillfully. *Shavasana,* the corpse position, is the beginning of the training in the art of "*ichha mrityu*" or voluntary death. There are certain internal, mental procedures, certain concentrations that are done by the yogi in *shavasana,* and they are in each step more complex... connecting to the subtle body, connecting to the *pranamayakosha,* and that *kosha* that becomes your identity. Very soon, *shava asana* is successful, you are not aware of the body. Only then is it *shava asana.* So there again you realise, without an awareness of the body, there is awareness, there is a consciousness or a life force. When the devotee (*sadhaka*) is in that state, he or she realizes, "I am." It is a whole different more pleasant direction, more pleasant dimension of my being. So this is the third way of dying.

SAMDONG RINPOCHE
ON BUDDHIST PERSPECTIVE OF DEATH (video clip)

The fourth and fifth ways are the actual permanent departure from the body. It happens in two ways. If the disciple is not well trained then he needs the guru's presence and help to be there and gently guide the consciousness out of his body.

One who is a master himself does not need that. In the *Upanishads* it is said, one should extend one's *prana,* the living force in the body (*svaat shariraat pravarihet munja iva*). The word there is not, "take it out", or "pull it out". It means "extend it" from one's body, patiently, gently, "like a fibre", from the "*munja*" plant. The reference to the fibre is to the subtle centre. There are 101 "*nadis*" figuratively. Texts speak of three *nadis,* sometimes 10, 14 and 1,25,000. One *nadi* that leads one upwards, takes one's entire consciousness onto that subtle channel and takes it out. That is the fifth kind of dying.

These are the five categories. Unfortunately those who have not taken to the path of personal spiritual realisation, no matter how religious, they are even the very learned who know all the *shastras,* even they remain afraid and obsessed with this fear but there is no cause to fear it.

According to the Buddhist perception, death is only the change of body, the continuum of consciousness. The consciousness goes from this body at the time of death, and takes a different kind of body.

Bordo Thodal is a treatise that is specially written to help dying people. They are bound to enter into an intermediary stage. After death, the consciousness leaves the present life body but is not immediately able to take the next life body; there is a need of an in-between period. In this transition period the consciousness takes a body of mental form. The mind does not have a gross body; it has a very subtle energy on which the consciousness depends. That consciousness takes another body in its next life when the intermediary stage is complete. This stage is very important for what kind of rebirth would be taken by the dead person. Bordo Thodal is always trying to educate dying people when they are entering into the intermediary stage, what it is like, and how one can realize who one is at that stage.

This is the transitional period. Of course there is some inconvenience, or feeling of misery to disintegrate the consciousness from the physical body and take a new physical body is a great transitional period. A kind of pain and misery will naturally come. But that should not be the cause of fear as it is today.

Nadi Jacket

In many cultures, the body is not viewed as a physical assemblage of flesh and bones, nor it is considered as a bag containing chemical processes. In many cultures, the mind is not considered to be located in the cranium. For example in yogic philosophy, intelligence as potential energy resides at the base of the spine and with progressive illuminations energy currents flow upward through the psychic centres, the *chakras* along the spine. The e-jacket, through built-in LED displays, illustrates alternative notions of the body found in yogic thought.

DEEPAK CHOPRA
DEATH as CREATIVE (video clip)

What is really death? Death is a quantum creative leap of the soul. It is a true act of creativity. You take the *karma*, the memories, the desires, the meanings, the relationships, the context, and the archetypal themes of a particular lifetime, you exhaust the creativity from those contexts, meanings and archetypal themes for that particular lifetime...the soul takes a period of incubation in the virtual domain, and then it has a quantum creative insight of creativity. It says, "How can I take those contexts, meanings, relationships and archetypal themes and jump from this location in space-time to this body-mind experience, with no transition in between." It is truly a quantum leap. And, of course, very simplistically, almost too simplistically, it is called reincarnation. What reincarnates is the contexts, meanings and relationships and archetypal themes of that particular soul.

The physical body as we experience it in our everyday normal waking stage of consciousness is actually a perceptual distortion, so what you are experiencing as a physical body is really an illusion; there isn't such a thing. It is the way it is imagined by consciousness and then experienced by consciousness. If you could see the body through the eyes of a modern physicist for example, you'll see that the body is made up of atoms. The atoms, in turn, are subatomic particles that are moving at lightning speed around huge empty spaces. And the subatomic particles, in turn, are fluctuations of energy and information in a huge void. They are not material things. Even though we call them particles they are actually waves of information and energy. So looking through the eyes of a modern physicist the body is proportionately as void as intergalactic space. If you could see it with divine eyes, in chapter 11, Krishna tells Arjuna: "Let me give you divine eyes so you can really see me as I am." He's talking about quantum senses if you were. The way a modern physicist would experience the body would be that you would see a huge emptiness, and a few scattered dots and spots, and some random electrical discharges in a universe of these fluctuations of information and energy. The information that structures your physical body, the information itself is moving at the speed of light, that is 1,86,000 miles per second or 3,00,000 km per sec. So when I go to a movie for example, I know that even though I see continuity in a movie, when I go to the projection room then I see still frames with gaps in between them, and in fact what is being projected is also still frames with gaps

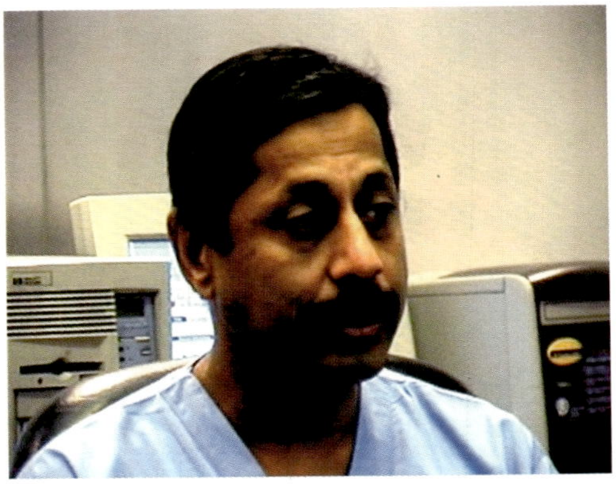

Dr. NARESH TREHAN (video clip) on MEDICAL DEATH

in between them. In fact people who are watching this programme right now, they are seeing continuity on their screens...but there is no continuity because these are flashes of images with gaps in between, but you move them at 24 frames per second and the human eye cannot process that so it imagines continuity, So too we live in a fluctuating universe which is appearing and disappearing at the speed of light, your body, my body is appearing and disappearing ...it's a dance of light, the whole universe is a dance of light and we imagine the dance of light to be a physical phenomenon. It's totally a perceptual distortion, just like the earth appears flat but it's not. The ground appears stationary but it is spinning at dizzying speed and hurtling through space at thousands of miles per hour. The body appears to be 3D, solid, having smell, texture and all the experiences we have through our senses, but none of them is real.

What stuns us the most is that it (the body) is such a perfect machine, such a complicated machine; I don't think that with all the science that is available today we have actually scratched the surface. It's less than one per cent of the mystique of the body we know. There are millions and millions of its methodologies and functions that we don't know about. No matter how savvy we may be or how authoritative we may sound there is a lot of ignorance about the human body still. The mechanism with which the body is found is very well described. It starts from what we call mitosis. Mitosis is the division of cells. Say, you take one sperm, fertilize the ova, and the cells unite. A nucleus is formed, it starts dividing...and can you imagine this one little cell differentiates itself...something will become a nose and an eye; their functions are totally different. It's the most fascinating machine. Can you ever imagine creating a machine like this?

No matter how much science or computer power we have generated, or robots we may have invented...the human body is such that we don't know a zillionth of its functions. How does this one cell that looks the same divide itself into billions of cells and each one of them has its own functions.

The eye itself has over a hundred parts. That's what I'm saying...you try to explain all this. How do you explain it?

One of the weaknesses of modern science is that scientists become so scientific, we lose track of other factors that may be influencing the healing of the body. Privately, of course, we may have our beliefs, but as an official statement, there is no such thing as life after death. There is a very cut and dry definition of death—it's over, it doesn't work anymore. The machine died.

I personally believe that there is a step above science because it doesn't make sense without it. Everybody is searching, so am I.

RANJIT NAIR
on PHYSICS and DEATH (video clip)

An interesting aspect of the relationship between physics and death came about through the atom bomb. This is the first atomic test explosion in Los Almagaldor where you have Oppenheimer with General Lesley Grove. And seeing this first atomic explosion's mushroom cloud rise, Oppenheimer is supposed to have quoted a stanza from the *Bhagwadgita,* which is translated as "I am become death, destroyer of worlds."

But basically physicists have thought that they have a power over life and death in a dramatic way and Oppenheimer himself said that "now physicists have known sin and this is a knowledge that they cannot lose." So the power of mega death if you will, rose as a result of the atomic bomb... As far as life and its inner value is concerned, physicists have very little to say about it, because their vision and attention is transfixed on the outer world. But they are certainly in a position to inflict death as well as prevent it.

Recycling of the Elements, Installations.

The Crossing, Installations.

SELECT BIBLIOGRAPHY

Bernier, Francois. *Travels in the Mogul Empire AD 1956-1968.* Translated by A. Constable and ed. revised by V.A. Smith. London: Oxford University Press, 1914.

Bharati, Agehananda. "Pilgrimage in the Indian Tradition," in *History of Religions*, 3, no. 1 (1963): 135-67.

Bhardwaj, Surinder Mohan. *Hindu Places of Pilgrims in India.* Berkeley: University of California Press, 1973.

Bhattacharya, B.C. *The History of Sarnath or the Cradle of Buddhism.* Banaras: Tara Printing Works, 1924.

Brown, J. S. and Duiguid, P. "Borderline Issues, Social and Material Aspects of Design," in *Human Computing Interaction,* 1993.

Callewant Winand M., Peter G. Fried Lander. *The Life and Works of Ravidas,* New Delhi: Manohar Publishers, 1992.

Chandra, Moti. *Kasi ka Itihas.* Bombay: Hindu Granth-Ratnakar, 1962.

Coomaraswami, A. K. *Yaskas : Essays in the Water Cosmology.* Edited by Paul Schroeder. New Delhi: Oxford University Press, 1993.

Danileou, Alain. *Hindu Polytheism.* New York: Pantheon Books, 1964.

Eck, Diana L. *Banaras : City of Light.* Lussane: Alfred A. Knopf, 1982.

Eck, Diana L. "India's Tirthas," in *History of Religions,* XXI, pp. 323-44; "Kasi, City and Symbol," in *Purana*, XX, ii, 1978.

Ganga Lahari by Pandit Jagannatha. Commentary by Sadashiva. Trans. Ima Scotsman. Delhi : Nag Publishers, 1999.

Gold, R. "The Future of Reading Exhibit," Xerox PARC, 2002; reviewed in *www.idonline.com/imdr01/readingwall.html* et. al. "XFR exhibit, Tech Museum, San Jose: Tech Museum, 2000."

Gonda, Jan. *Vishnuism and Sivaism: A Comparison.* London: University of London, The Athlone Press, 1970.

Greaves, Edwin. *Kashi: The City Illustrious or Benares.* Allahabad: The Indian Press, 1999.

Ishii, H. and Ullmer, B. *"Tangible Bits: Towards Seamless Interfaces between People, Bits and Atoms,"* Conference on Human Factors and Computing Systems,Toc 1997, Atlanta, New York : Atlanta ACM Press, 1997.

Kane, P.V. *History of Dharmasastra.* Government Oriental Series B. 6 Poona: Bhandarkar Oriental Research Institute, 1930-62, 2nd ed., 1973-74.

Kane, P.V. *History of Dharmasastra.* Vol. IV, Poona: Bhandarkar Oriental Research Institute, 1953.

Kasi Mrita Moksa Vicara by Suresvara. Edited by Gopinath Kaviraj. The Princess of Wales Saraswati Bhavana Text No. 67. Allahabad: Government Printing, 1936.

Kasi Rahsya (Brahmavaivarta Purana Parisista). Gurumandala Granthamalaya No. XIV, Vol. III. Calcutta: 1937.

Khanna, Madhu. "Representing Banaras, Living, Dying and Transformation : The Crossing Project" in *Evam, Forum on Indian Representations.* Edited by Makarand Paranjape 1: 1 & 2 (2002), pp.57-72.

Kramrisch, Stella. *Manifestations of Shiva.* Philadephia. : Philadelphia Museum of Art, 1981.

Kramrisch, Stella. *The Presence of Siva.* Princeton, New Jersey: Princeton University Press, 1981.

Linga Purana Trans., "Board of Scholars" and edited by J.L. Shastri, 2 vols. Ancient Indian Traditions and Mythology Series 5-6. Delhi: Motilal Banarsidass, 1973.

Makkuni, R. "The Crossing: Living, Dying and Transformation in Banaras, a Cultural Learning Project for the Next Millennium," in *Xerox PARC Report,* 1998.

Makkuni, R. Living Documents for Knowledge Capture and Learning. *Xerox PARC Report*, 1998; also published in the *UNESCO World Cultural Report*, 2000.

Mani, Vettam. *Puranic Encyclopaedia: A Comprehensive Dictionary with Special Reference to the Epic and Puranic Literature.* Delhi: Motilal Banarsidass, 1975.

Narada Puran. Ganesh Vasudeo Tagre. Translated and annotated. Part 1-4. Delhi: Motilal Banarsidass, 1980, 1981, 1982.

Neville, H.R. *Benares: A Gazetter.* District Gazetters of the United Provinces of Agra and Oudh, Vol. XXVI. Allahabad: Government Press, 1909.

O'Flaherty, Wendy Doniger. *Asceticism and Eroticism in the Mythology of Siva.* London: Oxford University Press, 1973.

Pandey, Raj Bali. *Hindu Samskaras.* and rev, ed. Delhi: Motilal Banarsidass, 1969.

Parry Jonathan P. "Death and Cosmogony in Kashi," in *Contributions to Indian Sociology* 15 (1981).

Parry Jonathan P. "Death and Cosmogony in Kashi," in Rana P.B. Singh, ed. *Banaras (Varanasi) Cosmic Order, Sacred City, Hindu Tradition's.* Varanasi : Tara Printing, 1993: 103-21.

Parry, Jonathan P. *Death in Banaras.* Cambridge: Cambridge University Press, 1994.

Purano me Ganga (in Hindi), ed. Daya Shankara, Dube. Trans. Ramapratap Tripathi. Prayaga: Hindu Sahitya Sammelana, Vikram Samvat, 2001.

Puri B. N. *Cities of Ancient India.* Meerut: Meenakshi Prakashan, 1966.

Rao T.A. Gopinatha. *Elements of Hindu Iconography.* 2 vols, each of 2 parts, 2nd ed. Delhi: Motilal Banarsidass, 1968.

Saraswati, Baidyanath. *Kashi: Myth and Reality of a Clasical Cultural Tradition.* Shimla: Institute of Advanced Studies, 1975.

Singh, Rana P.B. Ed. *Banaras (Varanasi) Cosmic Order, Sacred City, Hindu Traditions.* Varanasi : Tara Book Agency, 1993.

Singh, Rana P.B. "Sacred Geometry of India's Holy City, Varanasi: Kashi as Cosmo-gram," in *National Geographical Journal of India* vol. 40, 1994: 189-216.

Siva Purana, Trans. "A Board of Scholars," and edited by J.L. Shastri, 4 vols. *Ancient Indian Tradition and Mythology Series* 1-4 Delhi: Motilal Banarsidass, 1973.

Srimadvalmikiya Ramayana of Maharishi Valmiki, vols. 1 and 2. Gorakhpura: Gita Press.

Sukul, Kuber Nath. *Kasi Ke Yatrakrama.* Varanasi: Ram Ugraha Pandey. n.d.

Sukul, Kuber Nath. *Varanasi Down the Ages.* Varanasi: Bhargava Bhushan Press, 1974.

Sukul, Kuber Nath. *Varanasi ka Adhidavik-Vaibhava.* Varanasi Sri Mahesvari Press, 1968.

Sukul, Kuber Nath. *Varanasi Vaibhava,* Patna: Bihar Rastrabhasa Parisad, 1977.

Swami Sivanada, *Mother Ganga,* Shivanandanagara (Tehri-Garhwal): The Divine Life Society, 1994.

Tavernier, Jean Baptiste, *Travels in India.* Translated by V Ball. 2 vols. London: Macmillan, 1889.

The Linga Purana. Edited by J.L. Shastri. Trans. by a Board of Scholars. 2 vols . *Ancient Indian Tradition and Mythology,* vols. 3-6, Delhi: Motilal Banarsidass, 1973.

The Markandeya Purana. Translated by F. Eden Pargiter. Bibliotheca Indica, Calcutta: Asiatic Society, 1904.

The Skanda Purana Book IV *Kashi Khanda* Trans. G.V. Tagre, Delhi: Motilal Banarsidass, 1996.

The Sri Mad-Bhagvatam Translated by J.M. Sanyal. New Delhi: Munshiram Manoharlal, 1973.

Tripathi, Narayana Pati. *Kasi Yatra.* Vishvavidyalaya-rajatajayanti-granthamala, Varanasi : Sampurananda University, 1991.

Tripathi, Ram Sankar. *The Chequered History of the Golden Temple of Kashi Vishwanath, Kasi,* n.d.

Twain, Mark. *Following the Equator, A Journey Around the World.* Hartford: The American Publishing Company, 1898.

Upadhyaya, Baladeva. *Kashi ki Panditya Parampara* (1200-1980) (in Hindi) Varanasi: Vishvavidyalaya Prakashana, 1994.

Vaudeville, Charlotte. *Kabir.* Oxford: Oxford University Press, 1974.

Vidyarthi, L.P., Saraswati B.N., and Jha, Makan. *The Sacred Complex of Kashi.* Delhi: Concept, 1979.

Vijaya Das, Jaya. *Our Merciful Mother Ganga.* New Delhi: Pada Yatra Press, 2000.

Want, R., Fishkin K., Gujar, A., Harrison, B. "Bridging Physical and Virtual Worlds with Electronic Tags," *Xerox PARC Report,* CHI 99, 1998.

Zimmer, Heinrich. *The Art of Indian Asia—Its Mythology and Transformations.* 2 vols. Bollingen Series XXXIX. Princeton: Princeton University Press, 1955.

THE CROSSING PROJECT WINNING TEAM

PROJECT DIRECTOR
Ranjit Makkuni

PROJECT SCHOLAR
Dr. Madhu Khanna

TECHNOLOGY TEAM
Embedded Systems
Mustafa Siddiqi, Muralidhar Swarangi, Asif Abrar, Mark Yim, Kimon Roufas, David Duff, Scott Minneman, Dale McDonald-PARC - RED.

GRAPHIC PROGRAMMING
Tarun Jung Rawat, Pallab Chakraborty, Baishakee Sengupta, Puneet Monga, Pashim Tiwari, Vishesh Verma, Misha Gurnanee.

CONTENT TEAM
SCHOLARS
Ram Shankar Tripathi, Anand Krishna, Sam Dong Rinpoche, Rana P B Singh, Vidya Niwas Mishra, K D Tripathi, G N Mishra, Vagisha Shastri, Shuka Deo Singh, Swami Ved Bharati, Lokesh Chandra, Banushankar Mehta, Ananda Swami, Subhash Kak, Ranjit Nair, Vachaspati Upadhyaya, Zeena Sorabji, Makarand Paranjpe, Krishna Kant Shukla, Swami Mahadeva Nanda, Madhu Khanna, Satkari Mukhopadhyaya, Gopichand Narang, Sadhvi Bhavyananda, Rajiv Vora, Afaq Siddiqi, Kailash Vajpeyi, Deepak Chopra.

CONTRIBUTIONS
Naresh Trehan, Mark Tully, R P Sharma, Deepak Chopra, Puran Chandra, Prabhu Das, Mukund Lal, Shashank Singh, Veer Bhadra Mishra, Shrivatsa Goswami, Gaya Singh, Kamal Giri, Sadhvi Manorama, A B Singh, Gautam Bhattacharya.

PERFORMING ARTISTS
Kalanidhi Narayan, Kelucharan Mahapatra, Deepti Bhalla, Alarmel Valli, Priyadarshini Govind, Vikku Vinayakram, L K Pandit, Meeta Pandit, Durga Charan Mahato, Chau Troupe, Ranjit Makkuni, Mithilesh Jha, Ashish Sengupta, Naveen Kumar, Buntu, Arjun.

VISUAL ARTISTS
Venugopal, Jaya Chandran, Ashok Dilwali, Vijay Sharma, Late Chandrakala Devi, Giriraj Prasad, Kashinath, Nandan Lal, Rozalia Hummel, K P Umapathy, Jeet Ram, Babu Lal, Kalu Charana.

VIDEOGRAPHY
Kalpana Subramanian, Pallavi Arora, Ruchi Bakshi, Sreela Sarkar.

ADDITIONAL VIDEO FOOTAGE
Paul Taylor, Ein Lall.

CAMERA
Apal Singh, Subhash Day, Supavitra Babul, Sudhir Aggarwal, Sanjay Aggarwal, Alphonse Roy, Kalpana Subramanian, Ruchi Bakshi, Pallavi Arora, Rajgopal Mishra, N Devarajan.

VIDEO PRODUCTION
Pankaj Bhakuni, Rohan Hatkar, Hridayanath, Vinod Kumar, Kuldeep Rawat, Kailash Arya, Sumit Wadhwa, Hitesh Bhatia, Flamingo Films, Wilderness Films, Delhi Bioscope Company.

DESIGN TEAM
Accessory, Apparel, Product Design
Tanveen Ratti, Abha Gupta, Deepa Verma, Shivanee Dutt, Anurag Sehgal, Pankaj Maskara, Shweta Varma, Mustafa Siddiqi, Mohd. Asif, Nand Kishore Collection, Vrindaban.

MANAGEMENT
Xerox DMO/PARC
Carlos Pascual, Herve Gallaire, John Seely Brown, Michael Paige, Mark Stefik, Per-Kristian Halvorsen, Dave Robson, Ric Dauval, Jule Limoli, Rajeev Batra, Richard Adamo, Pierre Nothard, Pedro Fabrega, Ranjit Makkuni.

ADMINISTRATION, COORDINATION
Muralidhar Swarangi, Sasikumar, Kanchan Sharma, K R Bala, Indrajeet Borkakoty, Neeraj Sharma, Patricia Sheehan, Mali Sarpangal.

ACKNOWLEDGEMENT - TECHNOLOGY RESEARCH

Roy Want, Beverly Harrison, Anuj Gujar, PARC-RED, Rich Gold, Dale MacDonald, Scott Minneman, Jagmeet Kwatra, Sudipto Mukherjee, Santanu Chadhury, Subashish Banerjee, Sumitra Dutta Ray, Pramod P K., Gaurav Garg - IIT Delhi, Santosh Sahoo, Deepak Gupta.

ACKNOWLEDGEMENTS - DESIGN

Ritu Jain, Amardeep Singh, Rajesh Gupta, Kamakshi Kaul, George Thomas, Shailan Parker, Raja Thomas, Saumitri Choudhary, Tania Sengupta, Paridhi Sahai, Mitali Ganguly, Ramji Lal Sharma, Misha Gurnanee.

ACKNOWLEDGEMENTS - CONTENT (MUSIC)

Ustad Ali Akbar Khan, Ranjit Makkuni - Sitar, Mithilesh Jha - Tabla, Sanjay Chaturvedi, Ashish Sengupta.

RESOURCE PERSONS IN BANARAS / ADDITIONAL RESEARCH

Dr. Kalyan Krishna, Jyoti Shankar, Rati Shankar, Nikhat Grewal, Niranjana & Sudakshana Unnikrishnan.

ACKNOWLEDGEMENTS - INSTITUTIONS

Xerox Delhi Software Services,
IIT-Delhi,
Archaeological Survey of India - Dr. Komal Anand,
National Institute of Fashion Technology Delhi - Professor Archana Shastri,
National Institute of Design, Ahmedabad,
Indira Gandhi National Centre for Arts, New Delhi,
Sangeet Natak Academy, New Delhi,
Dakshinachitra Heritage Village,
Madras Craft Foundation, Chennai,
Tantra Foundation, New Delhi,
Imperial Hotel, New Delhi,
Ghalib Academy, New Delhi,
Sanga Veda Vidyalaya, Varanasi,
Ramakrishna Mission, Varanasi,
Durga Kund Vridhashram, Varanasi,
Kashilabh Mukti Bhawan,
The Doms of Manikarnika Ghat,
Til Bhandeshwar Temple, Varanasi,
Kedar Temple, Varanasi,
District Magistrate, Varanasi,
Commissioner Varanasi - Manoj Kumar,
Kala Kammune, Varanasi.

ACKNOWLEDGEMENT - MUSEUMS

Bharat Kala Bhawan, Varanasi - T K Biswas,
National Gallery of Modern Art, Mumbai
India Habitat Centre - Alka Pandey
Asia Society, New york - Vishakha Desai, Helen Abbott, Chaya Duggal
OK Centre for the Arts, Linz - Martin Strum.

ADDITIONAL SUPPORTERS / WELL WISHERS

Sacred World Foundation, Unni Warrier, Deepak Chopra, T M Ravi, Atri Chatterji, The Flora Family Fund, Martand Singh, Melanie Beene, Peter Gabriel, Her Holiness Madhavi Ma, Shikha Mataji, Pandit Mahendra Pandey, Peeko Maharaj Singh, Diana Chace, Cynthia Hirschorn, Rand Castile, Khurshid Bandopadhyaya.

ACKNOWLEDGEMENTS - CATALOGUE

Miniature Paintings from the collection of Bharat Kala Bhawan, Benaras (pp. 48, 53, 54, 55, 56, 57, 58, 63, 107, 108, 112, 120.
Text on Cycle Jhalla (p. 30)- Kalpana Subramanian
Copy Editor - Sheela Bajaj.